Interaction Process and Chinese EFL Learners' Proficiency Development

Shanshan Gu

Interaction Process and Chinese EFL Learners' Proficiency Development

A Cognitive and Interactionist Approach

Shanshan Gu
School of Foreign Studies
Shanghai University of Finance and
 Economics
Shanghai
China

ISBN 978-981-10-6834-8   ISBN 978-981-10-6835-5 (eBook)
https://doi.org/10.1007/978-981-10-6835-5

Jointly published with Shanghai Jiao Tong University Press

The print edition is not for sale in China Mainland. Customers from China Mainland please order the print book from: Shanghai Jiao Tong University Press.

Library of Congress Control Number: 2017956338

© Shanghai Jiao Tong University Press and Springer Nature Singapore Pte Ltd. 2018
This work is subject to copyright. All rights are reserved by the Publishers, whether the whole or part of the material is concerned, specifically the rights of translation, reprinting, reuse of illustrations, recitation, broadcasting, reproduction on microfilms or in any other physical way, and transmission or information storage and retrieval, electronic adaptation, computer software, or by similar or dissimilar methodology now known or hereafter developed.
The use of general descriptive names, registered names, trademarks, service marks, etc. in this publication does not imply, even in the absence of a specific statement, that such names are exempt from the relevant protective laws and regulations and therefore free for general use.
The publishers, the authors and the editors are safe to assume that the advice and information in this book are believed to be true and accurate at the date of publication. Neither the publishers nor the authors or the editors give a warranty, express or implied, with respect to the material contained herein or for any errors or omissions that may have been made. The publishers remains neutral with regard to jurisdictional claims in published maps and institutional affiliations.

Printed on acid-free paper

This Springer imprint is published by Springer Nature
The registered company is Springer Nature Singapore Pte Ltd.
The registered company address is: 152 Beach Road, #21-01/04 Gateway East, Singapore 189721, Singapore

Contents

1	**Introduction**	1
	1.1 Background	1
	1.2 Rationale	2
	1.3 Aims of the Book	4
	1.4 Outline of the Book	6
2	**A Cognitive and Interactionist Approach to SLA**	7
	2.1 Rationale	7
	2.2 Input and SLA	8
	2.2.1 Evidence Types in Input	8
	2.2.2 Role of Input in SLA	10
	2.3 Interaction and SLA	13
	2.3.1 Position of the Book on Interaction	13
	2.3.2 Function of Interaction in SLA	14
	2.3.3 NF and SLA	16
	2.4 Output and SLA	20
	2.4.1 Output Hypothesis	20
	2.4.2 Functions of Output	21
	2.4.3 Psycholinguistic Basis of the Output Hypothesis	24
	2.5 Learners' Internal Mechanisms and SLA	26
	2.5.1 Attention and SLA	26
	2.5.2 Perception and SLA	30
	2.6 Summary	31
3	**Pespectives on Interaction Process in SLA**	33
	3.1 Perspectives on NF in SLA	33
	3.1.1 The Effects of Recasts in SLA	33
	3.1.2 Recasts and Negotiation Moves in SLA	39

	3.2	Perspectives on MO in SLA	41
		3.2.1 MO in Response to NF	42
		3.2.2 MO and L2 Development	43
	3.3	Perspectives on Learners' Internal Mechanisms in SLA	46
		3.3.1 Noticing in SLA	46
		3.3.2 Learners' Perception in SLA	49
	3.4	Perspectives on English Question Forms in Interaction-Based Research	51
	3.5	Summary	54
4	**Issues in Research Methodology**		**57**
	4.1	Objectives	57
	4.2	Operationalization of EFL Development	58
	4.3	Research Design	59
		4.3.1 The Pretest	60
		4.3.2 The Treatment	60
		4.3.3 The Posttests	62
	4.4	Participants	62
		4.4.1 The EFL Learners	62
		4.4.2 The Instructors as Competent Interlocutors	63
	4.5	Instruments	64
		4.5.1 Tasks Employed	64
		4.5.2 Measurement of Perception	65
		4.5.3 Measurement of Noticing	66
		4.5.4 Questionnaires Employed in the Study	66
	4.6	Procedures	66
	4.7	Treatment of the Data	68
		4.7.1 Data Transcription	68
		4.7.2 Data Categorization	69
		4.7.3 Data Scoring	69
		4.7.4 Data Processing	70
5	**Effects of Interaction Process on EFL Development**		**71**
	5.1	Effects of Negative Feedback, Modified Output, Attention on EFL Development	71
		5.1.1 Data Input in SPSS	72
		5.1.2 Treatment Task Data Analysis	72
		5.1.3 Test Data Analysis	74
		5.1.4 Summary	88
	5.2	Effects of Learners' Perceptions on EFL Development	89
		5.2.1 Data Input in SPSS	89
		5.2.2 The EFL Learners' Perception About NF	89

		5.2.3	The EFL Learners' Perception About NF and Question Development........................	96
		5.2.4	Summary	98
	5.3	Interaction Process and Foreign Language Development........		99
		5.3.1	MO and EFL Development	99
		5.3.2	Attention and EFL Development	102
		5.3.3	NF and EFL Development......................	104
		5.3.4	Perceptions About NF and EFL Development	107
		5.3.5	Interactional Processes and EFL Development..........	110
6	**Conclusion and Implications**.............................			113
	6.1	Summary...		113
	6.2	Implications...		116
		6.2.1	Theoretical Implications...........................	116
		6.2.2	Pedagogical Implications	118
		6.2.3	Methodological Implications.......................	119
	6.3	Limitations and Suggestions for Future Research		120

Appendix A: Test Items 123

Appendix B: Treatment Activities 131

Appendix C: Examples of Developmental Stages and Question Forms............................... 135

Appendix D: Learning Fournal 137

Appendix E: Questionnaire 1.................................. 139

Appendix F: Exit Questionnaire (Questionnaire 2)................ 141

Appendix G: A Consent Form for Participation.................. 145

Appendix H: Instruction for Stimulated Recall 147

References 149

Abbreviations

CR	Clarification Request
EFL	English as a Foreign Language
ESL	English as a Second Language
FL	Foreign Language
FLT	Foreign Language Teaching
FonF	Focus on Form
L1	First Language
L2	Second Language
MO	Modified Output
NF	Negative Feedback
NNS	Non-native Speaker
NS	Native Speaker
PC	Perception Category
QD	The Final Judgment of Question Development in the Experiment
QD1	Question Development in the Immediate Posttest
QD2	Question Development in the Delayed Posttest
RA	Reported Attention
SLA	Second Language Acquisition
SPSS	Statistical Package for the Social Sciences
UG	Universal Grammar

List of Figures

Fig. 2.1	Levelt's speech production model (Levelt 1989: 9)	25
Fig. 5.1	Example of SPSS data input subject by subject	73
Fig. 5.2	SPSS data input group by group	73
Fig. 5.3	Comparison of EFL question development among groups	76
Fig. 5.4	Observed groups and predicted probabilities based on QD	81
Fig. 5.5	Observed groups and predicted probabilities based on QD1	85
Fig. 5.6	Observed groups and predicted probabilities based on QD2	87
Fig. 5.7	Perception data input in SPSS of the second group	90
Fig. 5.8	A model of SLA (Gass 1988: 200)	111

List of Tables

Table 5.1	Treatment task performance of each group	73
Table 5.2	Kruskal-Wallis test of the difference of the NF between groups	74
Table 5.3	Mann-Whitney test of the difference of the MO between groups	75
Table 5.4	Subjects of each group question development in the two posttests	75
Table 5.5	Correlation tests between recast and QD	77
Table 5.6	Correlation tests between CR and QD	77
Table 5.7	Correlation tests between RA and QD	78
Table 5.8	Correlation tests between MO and QD	78
Table 5.9	Correlation coefficients among variables based on QD	79
Table 5.10	Variables not in the equation based on QD (block 0: beginning block)	79
Table 5.11	Omnibus tests of model coefficients based on QD (Block 1: Method = Enter)	79
Table 5.12	Model summary based on QD	80
Table 5.13	Hosmer and Lemeshow test based on QD	80
Table 5.14	Prediction of logistic regression model based on QD	80
Table 5.15	Variables in the equation based on QD	81
Table 5.16	Correlation coefficients among variables in immediate posttest	82
Table 5.17	Variables not in the equation based on QD1 (block 0: beginning block)	83
Table 5.18	Omnibus tests of model coefficients based on QD1 (block 1: Method = Enter)	84
Table 5.19	Hosmer and Lemeshow test based on QD1	84
Table 5.20	Prediction of logistic regression model based on QD1	84
Table 5.21	Variables in the equation based on QD1	85
Table 5.22	Correlation coefficients among variables in delayed posttest	86

Table 5.23	Variables not in the equation based on QD2 (block 0: beginning block)	86
Table 5.24	Omnibus tests of model coefficients based on QD2 (block 1: method = enter)	86
Table 5.25	Hosmer and Lemeshow test based on QD2	86
Table 5.26	Prediction of logistic regression model based on QD2	87
Table 5.27	Variables in the equation based on QD2	88
Table 5.28	The EFL learners' perception about recasts group 2	91
Table 5.29	Paired samples test of PC in group 2	91
Table 5.30	The EFL learners' perception about CRs in group 3	92
Table 5.31	Paired samples test of PC in the group 3	93
Table 5.32	The EFL learners' perception about recasts + CRs in group 4	93
Table 5.33	Paired samples test of PC in group 4	94
Table 5.34	ANOVA analysis between groups	95
Table 5.35	Test of homogeneity of variances	95
Table 5.36	Multiple comparisons by post Hoc tests	96
Table 5.37	Chi-square tests of PC1 and QD	97
Table 5.38	Chi-square tests of PC2 and QD	97
Table 5.39	Chi-square tests of PC3 and QD	98

Chapter 1
Introduction

1.1 Background

The 1990s witnessed the resurgence of grammar teaching, the role of which in second language acquisition (SLA) had been ignored since the late 1970s. Research since 1990s has shown that grammar teaching is necessary for learners to attain high levels of proficiency in the target language (Nassaji and Fotos 2004: 126). The role of grammar teaching has become a focus of recent studies (e.g., DeKeyser 2005; Nassaji and Fotos 2004). Nassaji and Fotos (2004) reviewed research in support of grammar teaching, and pointed out four reasons for the reconsideration of grammar as a necessary component of language teaching from theoretical and empirical aspects.

Firstly, "the 1980s hypothesis that language can be learned without some degree of consciousness has been found problematic" (ibid.: 127) as Schmidt (1990, 1993, 2001) has emphasized that the role of conscious attention to form, "noticing" as he called, is necessary for language learning (cf. Leow 1998, 2001; Tomlin and Villa 1994). Secondly, it has been found that "L2 (second language) learners pass through developmental sequences" (Nassaji and Fotos 2004: 128), so teaching of grammar can influence developmental sequences of linguistic proficiency if the instruction accords with the learners' readiness to develop to a higher stage of sequences (Lightbown 2000). Thirdly, a large number of studies have demonstrated "the inadequacies of teaching approaches where the focus is primarily on meaning-focused communication, and grammar is not addressed" (Nassaji and Fotos 2004: 128). Lastly, a large body of research has presented the "evidence for the positive effects of grammar instruction" (ibid.: 128).

Therefore, more and more researchers have not doubted the necessity of grammar teaching, while they are against the traditional presentation-practice pedagogy "which treats language as an object of learning and has consisted of grammar lessons in which grammatical structures are explicitly presented by the teacher in a decontextualized manner" (Nassaji and Fotos 2004: 129). The point is to investigate how much and what type of grammar teaching is effective for SLA or foreign language teaching (FLT). This book is just generated with such a background.

1.2 Rationale

This book intends to investigate the impact of negative feedback (NF), learners' modified output (MO) in response to the feedback, learners' cognitive mechanisms, i.e., noticing and perception, on English as a foreign language (EFL) development. Pedagogically, the rationale for the book is dictated by how to manipulate focus-on-form (FonF) instruction through communicative interaction in FLT.

As aforementioned, it is the traditional grammar teaching pedagogy that is objected by researchers. A majority of researchers generally agree on a need for grammar teaching, but they still disagree on how to operationalize the instruction. For decades, researchers have done many investigations on approaches to grammar teaching. Ellis and his colleagues (2002) stated that learners did not achieve a very high level of linguistic competence from an entirely communication-based curriculum. For example, found that learners in French immersion programs across Canada with a highly communication-oriented curriculum failed to acquire such grammatical features as verb tense markings even after a very long period of study (Swain 1995). Spada and Lightbown (1993) also found a similar result from a study conducted in an intensive ESL program in Montreal with a highly communicatively-oriented curriculum. Based on these findings, Swain (1995: 141) has proposed that "a communicatively-oriented input-rich environment does not provide all the necessary conditions for second language acquisition", and attention to form is also necessary.

The question then arose how the learners' attention was guided to form. A lot of studies tried to answer the question. Norris and Ortega (2000) reviewed 49 studies on L2 instruction, in which focus was mainly placed on forms, characterizing traditional, synthetic approaches to grammar teaching involving discrete language elements. The review showed that the effectiveness of the instruction was impressively poor when it was measured in terms of learners' competence to use the targeted structures spontaneously in communication.

To resolve this problem, Long (1991: 45–46) has proposed an approach termed "focus on form", which "overtly draws students' attention to linguistic elements as they arise incidentally in lessons whose overriding focus is on meaning or communication"(cited from Doughty and Williams 1998: 3). For FonF instruction, the primary focus of attention is on meaning. Thus, it is obvious that this instruction is incorporated with communication. Long (1991) has also distinguished "FonF" from "focus on forms" for which the primary focus of attention is on the forms being targeted in isolation (cf. Doughty and Williams 1998; Ellis et al. 2002; Nassaji and Fotos 2004). As Doughty and Williams (1998) has stated, the advantage of FonF instruction over the focus on forms instruction is the cognitive processing support

1.2 Rationale

employed in FonF instruction, during which the learners' attention is guided right to a linguistic feature for the need of communication. Only in this way can attention to form be made compatible with the immutable processes that characterize L2 acquisition and thereby overcome persistent developmental errors (Ellis et al. 2002: 422). In recent research FonF instruction has been widely advocated by researchers (e.g. Doughty and Williams 1998; Ellis 2001; Ellis et al. 2002; Fotos 1998; Sheen 2003) in spite of the controversy over the issue. The challenge is to identify how to manipulate FonF instruction to promote SLA or FLT. A growing body of research has investigated that issue from aspects of processing instruction, interactional feedback, focused grammar tasks, and collaborative output tasks. This book also attempts to shed light on how to manipulate FonF instruction.

Theoretically, the book is motivated by a need to have a better understanding of the relationship between interaction and learning. Interaction research "evolved from work by Hatch (1978) on the importance of conversation to developing grammar and from claims by Krashen (1985) that comprehensible input is a necessary condition for SLA" (Mackey 1999: 558). Although the importance of conversation in SLA has long been confirmed, it was then only regarded as a means of practicing the target language rules. Beginning from Hatch (1978) and later developed by a number of researchers (e.g., Gass and Varonis 1989; Long 1983a, 1996; Pica 1988) L2 research has focused on the role of interaction between a native speaker (NS) and a non-native speaker (NNS) and between two NNSs in L2 development. Along with this line of research, conversation is not only a means for practice but more importantly a means for learning to take place. As Gass (1997) stated, "conversational interaction in a second language forms the basis for the development of syntax; it is not merely a forum for practice of grammatical structures" (p. 104). Then researchers began to attempt to establish a link between interaction and subsequent learning, generally operationalized as change in linguistic knowledge.

According to Mackey and Gass's (2006) brief review about interaction research, the early studies of interactions between NNS-NS are descriptive in nature, and mainly focus on how conversations between L2 learners and NSs are structured. Researchers have attempted to show the difference of conversations with learners and with NSs. Such investigations have concerned the frequency, functions, and patterns of negotiation routines, as well as the function of comprehension in language learning. However, most of the early investigations have failed to present a direct relationship between input, interaction, and acquisition. Then, the ensuing research began to focus on the value and function of particular discourse patterns in order to establish a link between interaction and comprehension. Long (1983a, b) pointed out the importance of comprehension for L2 acquisition with the help of the discourse structure and the interactional modifications, and suggested that interaction should provide learners with opportunities to gain new linguistic knowledge. Thus comprehensible input was largely claimed as sufficient condition for learning to take place (e.g., Krashen 1985). However, Swain (1985) demonstrated the insufficiency of comprehensible input in the promotion of L2 syntactical development. Swain (1985, 1993, 1995) pointed to the necessity of comprehensible output and claimed that "through producing language, either spoken or written, language acquisition/learning may occur" (Swain 1993: 159). Meanwhile, some researchers began to emphasize the role of incomprehensible input rather than comprehensible input (e.g., Gass 1997; White 1987). White (1987) suggested that when learners were provided with incomprehensible input containing higher-level linguistic knowledge, their failure in comprehension should help them be aware of their problem area. Gass (1997) claimed that incomprehensible input might trigger learners' noticing of the gap between their interlanguage forms and the target language forms. Successively, from the mid-1990s, researchers began to try to demonstrate the role of interaction empirically, that is, to show a more direct relationship between interaction and subsequent L2 development. For instance, Gass and Varonis (1994) provided evidence for the positive effects of interaction on L2 development. Mackey (1999) also suggested that active participation in interaction was associated with L2 learning. Since then, learners' cognitive processes were also taken into consideration in dealing with the relationship between interaction and subsequent L2 development.

The theoretical developments concerning input, output, and learners' cognition were synthesized by Long (1996) in his updated Interaction Hypothesis, which purported that "negotiation for meaning, and especially negotiation work that triggers interactional adjustments by the NS or more competent interlocutor, facilitates acquisition because it connects input, internal learner capacities, particularly selective attention, and output in productive ways" (pp. 451–452). Therefore, interaction-based research aims to account for various aspects of interlanguage learning through learners' exposure to that language, their production of that language, and the feedback they receive on their production (Mackey and Gass 2006). The present study in the book, along the line of interaction-based research, attempts to further explore the relationship between interaction and learning, and to have a better understanding of the relationship between communication, acquisition, and learners' internal mechanisms mediating between them.

1.3 Aims of the Book

In light of the necessity to find out effective ways to conduct FonF instruction and to have a better understanding of the relationship between interaction and learning, the book aims to explore the effects of interactional modifications, learners' reaction and learners' cognitive mechanisms on Chinese EFL learners' interlanguage development.

Theoretically, because most of interaction-based research is carried out in the context of SLA, it is necessary to examine whether the findings in that context can also be corroborated in the context of Chinese EFL learning. Particularly, it is necessary to investigate the difference between L2 learning and foreign language (FL) learning in interaction-learning relationship, and to extend the current understanding of interaction-learning relationship to new context. Gass (1990),

1.3 Aims of the Book

considering internal and external variables to the learner, has suggested that there are not only quantitative and qualitative differences but also numerous similarities in L2 acquisition and FL learning. Ellis (1994) has also claimed that the difference of L2 and FL lies in their different functions in the community. L2 is recognized as a means of communication among members with some other language as their mother tongue, while a foreign language is generally learnt through classroom instruction. Given that the two language learning situations may lead to different learning processes or outcomes, a question has arisen what interaction-learning relationship can be found for Chinese EFL learners. Moreover, according to Mackey and Gass (2006: 171), having firmly established the interaction-learning relationship, researchers began to extend knowledge base to new contexts, linguistic forms and languages, and interpretation of feedback. Accordingly, the research focus has moved beyond the question of whether interaction plays a role in interlanguage development to exploring how it promotes development. This book intends to explore the paramount question as to how interaction facilitates interlanguage development from various but connected aspects, i.e., input, output, and learners' internal mechanisms. The related pre-assumption is as follows. When EFL learners make errors on the target linguistic form during task-based interaction, more competent interlocutors will provide NF to learners. The NF takes various forms which may function alone or in combination to modulate the opportunity for learners to modify their previous utterances. If learners can notice the NF, perceive it as corrective, and meanwhile have opportunities to produce MO, they will be more likely to develop to a higher level in target linguistic forms. If the pre-assumption can be corroborated through empirical study, it will contribute to the understanding of the interaction-learning relationship for Chinese EFL learners by addressing under what conditions EFL learners can make use of NF provided for them and then modify their problematic utterances to develop their interlanguage system.

Pedagogically, this book attempts to shed light on how to manipulate FonF instruction through task-based interaction in Chinese EFL classrooms. As aforementioned, NF, learners' MO in response to that feedback, and learners' internal mechanisms will all be examined. Needless to say, results of academic research cannot be applied directly to classroom teaching and learning. However, the results may bring us to consider some pedagogical problems. Firstly, the examination of NF will lead us to think what kind of NF can be adopted in EFL classroom teaching, how to effectively make use of NF to make learners be aware of their errors, how to correct learners' errors in the communicative context, and how to combine different types of NF to arouse learners' attention to the target linguistic forms, and how to provide learners with opportunities to do modification. Secondly, the examination of MO will push us to consider how to keep learners actively participating in interactional tasks, how to enhance the opportunity for learners to produce output, and how to negotiate with learners about the target language. Finally, the examination of learners' internal mechanisms will urge us to think over how to draw learners' attention to linguistic forms through communicative tasks, how to draw learners' attention to teachers' NF, how to make learners be aware of the difference between the target language forms and their own utterances, and how to help learners be aware of their errors through teachers' feedback.

1.4 Outline of the Book

This book consists of six chapters, that is, introduction, theoretical framework, literature review, methods, results and discussion, conclusion and implications. This chapter is a brief introduction of the book, providing the background, demonstrating the rationale, illustrating the aim, and finally presenting the outline of the book.

Chapter 2 is devoted to establishing a theoretical framework for the study of the book. It begins with a clarification for the research position, and then focuses on the discussion of input related issues in SLA. Subsequently, it addresses the interaction related issues with the ensuing step to illustrate output related issues. In succession, it discusses learners' internal mechanisms. The final section is a summary about the theoretical framework.

Chapter 3 presents a review of related literature, including research on NF in SLA, research on MO in SLA, research on learners' noticing and perception in SLA, research on English question forms in interaction-based studies, and finally a summary about what can be drawn from the survey and what remains to be done.

Chapter 4 is related with methodological issues. It begins with an introduction of objectives and research questions. The ensuing section addresses the operationalization of EFL development. After that, it introduces the research design, the participants, the instruments, the procedures, and finally the treatment of the data.

Chapter 5 presents and discusses the results in detail. It shows and demonstrates the effects of NF in the form of recast and clarification request (CR), MO, learners' noticing question forms and perceptions about NF on EFL question development.

Chapter 6 is a conclusion of the book. It begins with a summary of the findings, discusses the theoretical, pedagogical and methodological implications, and finally points out the limitations and provides some suggestions for future research.

Chapter 2
A Cognitive and Interactionist Approach to SLA

This chapter presents the theoretical background of this book concerning interaction-based accounts of SLA. It begins with an account of the theoretical position of the study in SLA. Section 2.2 brings an introduction of input and SLA, concerning issues of evidence types of input and the role of input in L2 development. Then, Sect. 2.3 deals with issues of interaction and SLA, consisting of theories related with interaction and accounts of NF provided through interaction. The ensuing Sect. 2.4 provides an introduction of output and SLA, illustrating the role of output in L2 development and the psycholinguistic basis of the Output Hypothesis. Successively, Sect. 2.5 presents an illustration of learners' internal mechanisms and SLA, emphasizing the role of attention and its related notion of noticing, and perception in L2 development. Finally, Sect. 2.6 provides a summary of the theoretical framework, and presents the argument of this book.

2.1 Rationale

Throughout the various theories regarding how learning takes place, two influential positions have been summarized as the nature and the nurture positions in general (Egi 2004; Gass 1997, 2003). The nature position refers to "the possibility that learners (whether child first language learners or adult second language learners) come to the learning situation with innate knowledge about language" (Gass 2003: 224–225). On the other side, the nurture position claims that "language development is inspired and conditioned by the environment, that is, the interactions in which learners engage" (ibid.: 225).

As for the nature position, the innate knowledge about language is claimed to be Universal Grammar (UG), which is regarded as an innate language faculty equipped within learners (at least children) from birth to limit their grammar shaping (Chomsky 1981). Thus, when the input does not provide the information of abstractions for language learning, UG can allow children to learn the language.

Accordingly, children may eventually acquire target language owing to UG in spite of impoverished input, which merely functions as a trigger to set language-specific parameters. Although there is widespread agreement on some sort of innately specified knowledge born within children, it is still controversial whether L2 learners have access to UG (cf. Bley-Vroman 1990; O'Grady 1996; Wolfe-Quintero 1996). On the other hand, the nurture position attributes children's and adults' language learning to linguistic environment to a large degree. Thus, input here is assigned a more important role in language representation formation. Nevertheless, the two positions are not only contrary to each other, but also complementary for each other. It is widely acknowledged that the human brain is equipped with some means in order to organize the language experiences presented to human beings in the course of their development (Braine 1994). As Wolfe-Quintero (1996: 338) pointed out, "there is a symbiotic, non-arbitrary relationship between the innate cognitive capacity for language learning and the input available in the environment, neither of which can be ignored". In this view, language learning is dynamic concerning not only how linguistic knowledge comes into being but also how language develops as a function of interactions in which learners are engaged. Gass (1997) has posited that the question is how innate knowledge interacts with the environment and input in the creation of linguistic knowledge.

Drawing on the contribution of the two positions in language learning, the book takes a cognitive and interactionist approach to SLA. According to Gleason (2005), the interactionist approach indicates that various factors affect the course of language development during which these factors are mutually dependent on, interact with, and modify one another. It also claims that language learning is stimulated by communicative pressure because "the conversational interaction provides learners with an acquisition-rich environment where they have access to comprehensible input, output opportunities, and interactional feedback" (Egi 2004: 6). Moreover, the cognitive perspective on SLA is interested in learners' internal mechanisms (e.g., attention, perception) that mediate between conversational interaction and acquisition. Therefore, the book takes a cognitive and interactionist approach to investigate the roles of various factors during the interactional process for L2/FL development.

2.2 Input and SLA

2.2.1 Evidence Types in Input

Input, as one of the language learning requirements, may provide learners with various types of evidence. According to Gass (1997, 2003), there are three types of evidence available to learners in the process of language learning (both L1 and L2): positive evidence, negative evidence, and indirect negative evidence. Indirect negative evidence will not be addressed below because it is the least relevant to interaction and the book does not concern this one.

2.2.1.1 Definition of Evidence Types

Positive evidence refers to the input and comprises the set of well-formed sentences to which learners are exposed (Gass 1997: 36). In general terms, positive evidence can take the form of either spoken language (or visual language in the case of sign language) or written language. According to Gass (1997, 2003), it is the most direct means for learners to form linguistic hypotheses. It is also regarded as models in SLA studies. According to Oliver (2000), positive evidence can be provided either as authentic input or as modified input or teacher talk.

In contrast, negative evidence refers to the type of information that is provided to learners concerning the incorrectness of an utterance (Gass 1997: 37). That is, NF provides information to learners about what is not possible in the target language (Oliver 2000). The incorrectness can be shown to learners explicitly or implicitly. If the negative evidence takes the form of explicit information, it will be direct information about the ungrammatical nature of the learner's utterance. If the negative evidence takes the form of implicit information it will be indirect information about the ungrammatical nature which must be inferred. In this case, it is probable that learners cannot understand the corrective nature of the implicit negative evidence.

2.2.1.2 Contribution of Evidence Types to SLA

The issue of evidence types in input was put forward from a theoretical linguistic perspective. The contribution of positive evidence is much clearer than negative evidence to SLA. According to Gass (1997, 2003), positive evidence, as the most obviously necessary requirement for learning, can provide learners with opportunities of exposure to a set of grammatical sentences for the target language learning to occur.

However, the significance of negative evidence is less clear either in L1 or L2. According to Gass (1997, 2003), in L1 acquisition negative evidence provides the basis of the innateness argument. It is because of lacking in correction in the learning environment, that there is a need for innateness. Moreover, even if such correction, when available for children, may inform them of the occurrence of errors, it may not show children how to correct the errors and how to revise their previous hypotheses. Similarly, in L2 acquisition, adults are assumed to have access to the same innate universal constraints or properties as children due to a lack of negative evidence. Nevertheless, different from the situation in L1, the assumption of lack of negative evidence in L2 acquisition is not warranted clearly (Gass 1997). Additionally, Schwartz (1993) has claimed that only positive evidence contributes to the formation and restructuring of L2 grammars, and also questions the role of negative evidence in the aspect of the extent to which negative evidence could engage UG.

It should be noted that although the researchers holding a nativist explanation of acquisition have claimed that positive evidence is all that is required for acquisition, the researchers holding an interactionist perspective have proposed a role for both positive and negative evidence. When learners are provided with information of negative evidence, they are likely to search for additional evidence for correction. It is necessary to find out whether negative evidence or positive evidence determines the change. White (1991), and Trahey and White (1993) examined the role of negative evidence and positive evidence respectively. The two studies have shown that both positive and negative evidence are beneficial in L2 learning. Positive evidence can present to learners the target language information whereas negative evidence can show ungrammatical nature of learners' output (Gass 1997). Furthermore, according to Oliver (2000), negative evidence can be provided preemptively or reactively. Reactive negative evidence highlights differences between the target language and learners' output and thus may benefit the target language learning. Because the role of negative evidence in SLA is still a contentious issue, it is necessary to reexamine the potential role of negative evidence in SLA by investigating the nature and structure of conversational interactions where negative evidence may be present, which has been expatiated in Sect. 2.3.

2.2.2 Role of Input in SLA

The study of the role of input in SLA has a long history, beginning from the early twentieth century. From then on input has been assigned an important role in SLA research by researchers in various views of language. Ellis (1994) distinguished three different views about the role of input, i.e., the behaviorist, the mentalist, and the interactionist.

The earliest conceptualizations of L2 acquisition, on the basis of a behaviorist view, rely heavily on the input provided to learners (Gass 2003). In this view, language learning is the consequence of stimulus-response and habit formation by way of imitation. With the disfavor of the behaviorist, the mentalist view regards input only as a "trigger" that sets off internal language processing (Gass 1997). In this view, the role of input is minimized. Different from the above two views, the interactionist view of language agrees on the important role of input within the constraints imposed by learners' internal mechanisms. In this view, the conversational interaction is also assigned an important role for language learning in making L2 salient to learners.

To date, the important role of input has not diminished, whereas what has changed is the conceptualization of how individuals process the input, and how the input interacts with the mental capacities of those learning a language (Gass 2003).

2.2.2.1 Input Hypothesis

The Input Hypothesis, developed by Krashen (1985), is the central part of the Monitor model in which the input plays a dominant role. "The Input Hypothesis claims that humans acquire language in only one way—by understanding message, or by receiving 'comprehensible input'" (Krashen 1985: 2). Comprehensible input is defined as "the message acquirer is able to understand", and is identified as "the essential ingredient in language acquisition" (Krashen 1985: 101). In other words, comprehensible input is considered as "bit of language that is heard or read and that contains language slightly ahead of a learner's current state of grammatical knowledge" (Gass 1997: 81). Krashen has also claimed that learners must be exposed to comprehensible input which contained language structures beyond their current level of interlanguage development called "i + 1" (1985: 2). When learners move from i, their current level, to i + 1, they should understand input containing i + 1, during which learners focus on the meaning and not on the form of the input. In that case, language learning can take place. Furthermore, as Gass (1997) has stated, Krashen assumed a language acquisition device, that is, an innate mental structure capable of handling both L1 and L2 acquisition. Although input can activate this innate mental structure, only input on the level of i + 1 can help to alter learners' grammar. In addition, Krashen (1985) regarded speaking as a result of acquisition but not as its cause because in his view input being understood was enough for the necessary grammar to be automatically provided. Therefore, Krashen's Input Hypothesis has assumed input to play a determinative role in SLA and only input on the level of i + 1 is related with SLA.

Although the Input Hypothesis can account for a wide variety of phenomena and has brought a great impact on SLA research, it has been criticized theoretically and empirically. Theoretically, Krashen's claim that comprehensible input actually causes acquisition is the subject of the criticism. Researchers (e.g., Trahey and White 1993; White 1987) have argued that comprehensible input is insufficient for L2 acquisition when learner hypotheses or L1 structures lead to L2 overgeneralization because it is impossible to revise their utterances on the basis of positive evidence alone. It is possible for learners to understand the meaning of the input beyond their grammatical knowledge, whereas it is impossible for learners to develop the input into grammatical acquisition only by comprehension. Thus, comprehension does not necessarily guarantee acquisition. Empirically, the insufficiency of comprehensible input has been shown by studies on the L2 achievement by learners in Canadian French immersion programs, reviewed by Swain (1985, 1995, 1998). The studies showed that immersion L1 French learners of English were found to perform comparably with NSs on listening and reading comprehension, but not on production measures. Even after continuous L2 exposure in the subsequent years of education, immersion learners were still found to make a wide variety of grammatical errors in production. Therefore, comprehensible input can never be sufficient for SLA. Krashen has overlooked the difference between input and intake and then has oversimplified the complex acquisition process.

Despite the inadequacies, the Input Hypothesis, however, should not be abandoned utterly because it has contributed to SLA research in drawing our attention to the role of input. Considering the significance of the Input Hypothesis, the book tries to take a more holistic view on input. That is, we regard input as one necessary component in language development in order to explore the role of input and the relationship between input and other components during interactional processes, such as learners' internal capacity, output, etc.

2.2.2.2 Input Processing

According to Gass (2003), a crucial question in understanding the role of input is related with processing. VanPatten (1995, 1996) has proposed a model of Input Processing, which deals with presentation, timing of input, and the elements which L2 learners focus on as they process input. In particular, it concerns the conversion of input to intake and specifically centers on form-meaning relations (Gass 1997). Crucial to the model of Input Processing is the assumption that human beings possess limited processing capacities (Izumi 2003). VanPatten and his colleagues' research is based on the concept of attention to form and its role in the process in which a learner moves from input to intake and then to output. It has been claimed that learners are not able to attend to all the information in the input, only some of which can be processed as the focus of attention (Gass 1997; McLaughlin 1987; Robinson 1995). In VanPatten's view, certain parts of input that are immediately relevant to the message content may tend to be attended. Certain principles are believed to guide the ways in which learners can process grammatical form in their attempt to comprehend input strings (Izumi 2003). L2 learners with limited processing capacities may firstly search the input for content words, and then the forms with high communicative value, and finally the forms with low communicative value only under the condition that their attentional resources are not consumed during the processing of forms. It is possible that learners may "never attend to purely formal, functionally redundant forms unless some form of instructional intervention forces them to do so (Izumi 2003: 179). In this sense, VanPatten's model of Input Processing connects the input with one of the learner's internal capacities, i.e., attention.

Moreover, VanPatten's model of Input Processing has prompted a wide range of studies to address how the input can facilitate learners' L2 development. According to Gass's (1997, 2003) review, in order to investigate how the input is processed and hence how an internalized system develops, VanPatten compared two instructional models: (a) a traditional grammar instruction in which grammatical information (i.e., input) was presented to the learner and then practiced, and (b) the input had been presented before an internalized system began to develop to change the way that input was perceived and processed. The results have indicated that there is a positive effect for the second instructional model over the first one. Then, in the examination of how explicit information benefits processing, VanPatten and Oikkenon's (1996) study, a replication study of VanPatten and Cadierno (1993), has shown that the beneficial effects of instruction derive from the structured input activities but not the explicit information. DeKeyser and Sokalski's (1996) study, another replication study of VanPatten and Cadierno (1993), investigated the effects of production versus comprehension activities. They have found a different result from the original studies, specifically in the fact that "practice at the level of input versus practice at the level of output differentially affected comprehension and production, with the former being better for comprehension and the latter for production" (Gass 2003: 232). This finding has suggested that the skills of comprehension and production are acquired separately. Another study on comprehension and production activities, conducted by Tomasello and Herron (1988, 1989), concerned retreating from overgeneralized errors. They have found that "the type of input that allowed corrective feedback to occur after the learner had made an error was more meaningful than input that attempted to prevent an error from occurring" (Gass 2003: 232). It indicated that the occurrence of errors and the appropriate feedback to errors have a greater likelihood of drawing learners' attention to the errors.

In sum, the model of Input Processing and the related empirical studies have addressed what kind of input is efficient in SLA, how input can facilitate SLA, and how input interacts with learners' internal capacities. It is assumed that input may work to facilitate L2 development under the circumstance that learners convert it into intake, i.e., something meaningful as part of the process of grammar formation. It is also assumed that different from comprehension of input, production, i.e., output, plays a substantive role in L2 development. Therefore, we may draw the conclusion that input is related with learners' internal capacity, such as attention, in terms of the aspect how input is converted into intake during conversational interaction, and that input and output may function differently in the process of L2 development.

2.3 Interaction and SLA

2.3.1 Position of the Book on Interaction

In general terms, interaction refers to the interpersonal activity that occurs during communication. According to Gass and Selinker (1993), when the flow of conversation is interrupted, participants negotiate what is not understood, that is, they may question particular utterances and/or request conversational help to compensate. Such negotiation of meaning is regarded as interaction, which consists of "those instances in conversation when participants need to interrupt the flow of the conversation in order for both parties to understand what the conversation is about" (Gass and Selinker 1993: 272). Then, in the early work focused on input, interaction refers to "the ways that proficient speakers (generally native speakers) modify their speech, presumably with the goal of making their speech comprehensible, to those with limited knowledge of the target language" (Gass 2003: 232). However, within that tradition, interactional structure was not investigated. After that, when research focus was shifted onto the interactional structure of conversation, the emphasis has been placed on the role which negotiated interaction between NSs and NNSs, and between two NNSs plays in L2 development (Gass 2003). The book, along this line of research, focuses on the role of the interactional structure of conversation in L2/FL development.

2.3.2 Function of Interaction in SLA

Long (1996) has addressed the function of interaction through the revised version of the Interaction Hypothesis, which takes as the starting point the notion that conversational interaction is the basis for L2 development rather than being only a way to practice language (Gass 2003). According to Mackey (1999), Long's Interaction Hypothesis (Long 1983a, b, 1985, 1996) evolved from Hatch's (1978) study on the role of conversation in developing grammar and from Krashen's (1985) claims on the role of comprehensible input for SLA. In the revised version of the Interaction Hypothesis, Long (1996: 451–452) stated:

> negotiation for meaning, and especially negotiation work that triggers interactional adjustments by the NS or more competent interlocutor, facilitates acquisition because it connects input, internal learner capacities, particularly selective attention, and output in productive ways.

Clearly, in a holistic perspective, negotiated interaction is supposed to integrate input, the learner, and output. Then interaction is assigned an important role as the means by which learning takes place. Long (1996: 414) also stated:

> it is proposed that environmental contributions to acquisition are mediated by selective attention and the learner's developing L2 processing capacity, and that these resources are brought together most usefully, although not exclusively, during negotiation for meaning.

It can be seen from the statement that the Interaction Hypothesis has accounted for how interaction contributes to language acquisition by specifying the learner's internal capacities. It indicates that input cannot be converted to output to facilitate language acquisition without learners' internal capacities, in particular, attention as a mediator through negotiated interaction. Moreover, the Interaction Hypothesis reveals that the conversational interaction is able to draw learners' limited attentional resources to a discrepancy between their interlanguage and the target language, and to new information about L2 not yet being acquired (Gass 2003). As Gass (1997, 2003) has stated, the conversational interaction may serve as a priming device, preparing the stage for learning to take place.

Long's Interaction Hypothesis has stimulated research into the role of interaction in SLA. A variety of empirical studies have examined the effects of different interactional conditions on L2 production and acquisition (e.g., Gass 1997; Gass et al. 1998; Gass and Varonis 1994; Mackey 1999; Pica 1994). Pica's (1994) comprehensive review of negotiated interaction has demonstrated that interaction may facilitate the necessary conditions and processes that are supposed to be important in L2 learning. Those conditions and processes can provide opportunities for learners to notice the form of the target language when linguistic units are rephrased, repeated, and reorganized to aid comprehension. Pica (1994) also showed how certain features of syntactic elements, being segmented or manipulated through interaction, could be made salient to learners by way of stress, intonation, and foregrounding. Furthermore, on the function of interaction, Gass (1997) has added that the effects of interaction may not be immediate, claiming that it is important to look for delayed developmental effects of interaction.

Among the studies on the function of interaction, the role of negotiation in SLA has also been emphasized by researchers (e.g. Gass 1997; Lyster 1998a, b; Pica 1992). Gass (1997) has noted that negotiation includes negotiation of form and negotiation of meaning, though they are not always easily separable. Pica (1992) examined the role of negotiation of meaning in L2 acquisition. Pica (1992: 200) regarded negotiation as a type of interaction through which "learners and their interlocutors adjust their speech phonologically, lexically, and morphosyntactically to resolve difficulties in mutual understanding that impede the course of their communication". Pica (1992: 205) has found that negotiation can provide learners with: "(1) L2 input adjusted or modified for their comprehension needs; (2) feedback on semantic and structural features of interlanguage; (3) opportunities to adjust, manipulate, or modify semantic and structural features of their interlanguage; and (4) a source of L2 data that highlights L2 semantic and structural relationship". The results have indicated that negotiation of meaning is always related with negotiation of form, that negotiation is able to result in interactional feedback, that negotiation is able to push learners and their interlocutors to modify their utterance either from semantic aspect or from structural aspect or from both, and finally that negotiation is able to establish form-meaning relationship. Pica's (1992) study is also quite an illustration of how interaction potentially facilitates L2 learners' interlanguage development.

Furthermore, more and more researchers began to investigate the role of negotiation of form in L2 learning. Long (1996) and Ellis (1985) have defined the types of negotiation of form. Lyster (1998a, b) coded corrective feedback (also called NF by many researchers, e.g. Ayoun 2001; Iwashita 2003; McDonough 2005) as negotiation of form, and identified the relationship among error types, corrective feedback types, and immediate learner repair. Morris (2002) examined the role of negotiation of form, categorized as NF, in pair work of adult learners of Spanish. Obviously, interaction research then began to focus on the effects of specific interactional feedback on L2 development. In particular, one common account has suggested that interaction may be beneficial because it provides learners with exposure to NF in response to their nontarget-like utterances (Gass 1997; Long 1996; Pica 1994). Long (1996) has specifically addressed the role of NF during conversational interaction. In the updated version of the Interaction Hypothesis, Long (1996: 414) stated:

NF obtained during negotiation work or elsewhere may be facilitative of L2 development, at least for vocabulary, morphology, and language-specific syntax, and essential for learning certain specifiable L1-L2 contrasts.

From the above statement it is clear that negotiated interaction may also facilitate L2 learning by eliciting NF in response to learners' nontarget-like utterances. In this case, NF can function by inducing learners' attention to the target language forms.

As aforementioned in Sect. 2.2.1, it is necessary to reexamine the potential role of negative evidence of input in SLA by investigating the nature and structure of conversational interaction where negative evidence may be present. Therefore, both the research on interaction and the research on input converge on the issue of identifying the effects of interactional feedback on L2 development. The present book intends to explore the useful types of input and the function of interaction through investigating the target language development and NF which has been illustrated in the following section.

2.3.3 NF and SLA

2.3.3.1 Definition of NF

NF relates to the issue of how competent speakers react to learners' language errors. It has been entitled a variety of terms according to the disciplinary orientation of the researcher. The various terms also indicate different research focuses and different data collection methods (Schachter 1991). As Lyster and Ranta (1997: 38) has noted, it was examined in terms of negative evidence by linguists, as repair by discourse analysts, as NF by psychologists, as corrective feedback by L2 teachers, and as focus-on-form in more recent work in classroom SLA. In this book, NF and corrective feedback are used interchangeably referring to the same concept. We have adopted Iwashita's (2003) definition of NF. According to Iwashita (2003: 2), "the term 'feedback' refers to some kind of NS response to what the learner has said; the feedback that learners receive during interaction can either be positive or negative. NF is an interlocutor's interactional move that indicates explicitly or implicitly any nontarget-like feature in the learner's speech".

2.3.3.2 Categorization of NF

Iwashita's definition indicates that in general terms NF can be divided into two categories, that is, explicit NF and implicit NF. According to Ellis (1985) and Long (1996), explicit NF is an overt error correction per se, while implicit NF usually takes the form of recasts or negotiation moves (i.e. confirmation checks, CRs and repetitions) that indicate to the learner that there is a problem with his output. Explicit NF is relatively infrequent in naturalistic interaction while implicit NF is

2.3 Interaction and SLA

more frequently provided (Mackey et al. 2003; Oliver 1995, 2000; Pica 1994). More researchers are interested in implicit NF because there is still controversy on the role of implicit NF, which is also within the consideration of the book.

Recasts, as a type of implicit NF, have aroused many researchers' interest. Recasts are defined as target-like reformulations of ungrammatical utterances that maintain the central meaning of the original utterance (Long 1996). There is an example of a recast in the instructor's response to the learner's ungrammatical utterance in (1).

(1) Learner: Why the man came to see his teacher?
    Instructor: Why did the man come to see his teacher? Well, because today is the woman's birthday. ...

(the data from the study in the book, Learner 26 in treatment 2 Task 2)

A CR refers to an interactional move in which a speaker solicits aid in understanding a partner's previous utterance by means of questions or statements of non-comprehension (Long 1996; Ellis 1985). The instructor's utterance in (2) is an instance of a CR.

(2) Learner: Does they're sister?
    Instructor: Sorry?
    Learner: What's the relationship between them?

(the data from the study in the book, Learner 34 in treatment 1 Task 2)

A confirmation check is defined as the repetition with rising intonation of all or part of a partner's previous utterance in an attempt to confirm that the message was understood correctly (ibid.). An example of a confirmation check is shown in the native speaker's response in (3) below.

(3) NNS: He have two bikes.
    NS: Have two bikes?

(the data from Morris 2002: 15)

A comprehension check refers to the response provided at the time when speakers attempt to verify that their immediately preceding utterance has been understood by their partner (ibid.). Typically a speaker uses a question to perform this function, as seen in turn 2 of Learner 3 in (4) below. The italic parts are translations of Spanish.

(4) Turn 1 Learner 3: El estres es mas o menos cuando tu estas en tu trabajo?
                     (The stress is more or less when you are in your job?)
    Turn 2 Learner 3: Comprendes?
                     (Do you understand?)

(the data from Bearden 2003: 17)

As for a repetition, the teacher repeats the ill-formed part of the student's utterance, usually with a change in intonation (Panova and Lyster 2002), as seen in (5) below.

(5) Teacher: …Here, when you do a paragraph, you start here, well let's see, anyway, you write …write, write, write (pretends to be writing on the board), remember this is … What is this called?
Student: Comma.
Teacher: Comma? (repetition)
Student: Period.

(the data from Panova and Lyster 2002: 584–585)

Although among researchers it is widely accepted that NF can be divided into explicit NF and implicit NF, the categorization and coding of implicit NF types during interaction are still problematic, because negotiation moves and recasts are not mutually exclusive categories (Mackey et al. 2003). Confirmation checks, for instance, generally regarded as negotiation moves, can also contain recasts (Leeman 2000; Mackey et al. 2003; Oliver 2000). The NS's utterance is such an example shown in (6) below:

(6) NNS: And I 'ave two-two cup.
NS: You have two cups?
NNS: Yeah.

(the data from Oliver 2000: 120–121)

Mackey et al. (2003) have noted that some studies attempt to differentiate among NF types based on interesting criteria, such as whether feedback includes the target form (Gass 1997; Leeman 2000, 2003), and whether feedback enhances the salience of the target form (Leeman 2000, 2003). As aforementioned in Sect. 2.3.2, Pica (1992) has found negotiation moves can provide learners with opportunities to modify their nontarget-like utterance. Swain (1985, 1995) has also assumed the importance of this pushed output. Additionally, researchers have found empirical evidence (Lyster 1998a, b; Lyster and Ranta 1997; Oliver 1995, 2000) that some types of feedback seem to promote MO, while some do not. Given all these, another way to categorize NF is whether the NF provides opportunities for MO (Mackey et al. 2003). The present study attempts to explore NF according to this criterion.

2.3.3.3 Role of NF in SLA

The issue of whether NF has effects on L2 development has become quite a concern of SLA researchers and FL teachers. It is necessary to have a systematic discussion about NF and SLA, that is, to confirm the availability of NF firstly, then to address the role of NF in L2 development, and finally to elucidate the reason why NF facilitates L2 development.

2.3 Interaction and SLA

Early studies have doubted whether NF actually exists at all and the argument about its existence is still alive up to the present day (e.g. Beck and Eubank 1991; Grimshaw and Pinker 1989; Marcus 1993). The doubt may stem from the fact that the focus of the early studies is explicit, not implicit NF, which is found to be largely ignored in early studies (Oliver 2000). For instance, in Chaudron's (1986, 1987) studies, although NF was not found in NNS-NS interactions, the feedback under investigation was explicit correction per se. Similar results have been found in several other studies (e.g. Chun et al. 1982; Day et al. 1984) which all regarded explicit correction as NF alone. Obviously, the definition of NF in early studies was too narrow. Therefore, it seems that the lack of support for the role of NF in early studies is due to the limitation of its definition.

In contrast, recent SLA research showed that implicit NF was indeed provided to and used by L2 learners (e.g., Chaudron 1977; Doughty 1994; Lyster 1998b; Lyster and Ranta 1997; Mackey et al. 2003; Morris 2002; Oliver 1995, 1998, 2000). Chaudron (1977) suggested that NF in the form of recasts was available to learners and they might incorporate the feedback in their subsequent turn under some conditions. Doughty (1994) found that learners did receive NF and some were able to recognize the correct forms in recasts and to make use of the information to formulate target-like utterances. Oliver (1998) also suggested the availability of implicit NF, particularly negotiation moves and recasts, in child (NNS-NNS and NNS-NS) dyads. Mackey et al. (2003) examined the provision and use of NF in both NS-NNS and NNS-NNS adult and child dyadic interactions. Their results did show that participation in task-based interaction was able to provide exposure to feedback in theoretically sufficient amounts.

However, these studies did not assess the potential role of NF in learners' L2 development. Employing pretest and posttest measures, recent experimental interaction studies have explored the precise effects of NF on L2 development (e.g. Ayoun 2001; Doughty and Varela 1998; Leeman 2000; Long et al. 1998; Mackey and Philp 1998). All these experimental studies have demonstrated the effects of NF, particularly recasts, on L2 development through NNS-NS or teacher-learner interactions in the context of the laboratory or the classroom, at least for some structures in some languages. The detailed review of these studies has been presented in Chap. 3.

Then how does NF facilitate L2 development? Muranoi (1996) has stated that from the cognitive perspective, NF is considered to be crucial in language learning, for it is a type of cognitive skill learning, requiring NF for hypothesis testing and especially for restricting overgeneralized rules (e.g. Anderson 1983; Cook 1993; Levelt 1978; McLaughlin 1987; Schachter 1991). Cook (1993: 264) made a brief and comprehensible summary of Anderson's language learning cycle as follows. Anderson (1983) has argued that NF is crucial in discovering the semantic and structural relationships of the target language, and has expatiated on the cycle. It has been claimed that learners firstly form a semantic base, and then transform the semantic base into a sentence according to the production rules they have already possessed. Then, NF on the correctness of the utterance is provided to learners so as to make them modify their production rules by formulating new ones and strengthening or dropping old rules. These new revised rules are beneficial for learners to form other semantic bases. Therefore, NF is crucial in this cycle of language learning. Moreover, according to Anderson's language learning cycle, NF functions in language learning by virtue of enabling learners to modify their production rules. In most studies on the availability of NF discussed previously (Chaudron 1977; Doughty 1994; Oliver 1995; Lyster and Ranta 1997; Oliver 2000; Morris 2002), learners' modification (also called reformulation or repair by some researchers) of their previous utterance has been found in response to NF, in particular, negotiation moves. In those studies NF are also considered to facilitate L2 development through pushing learners to produce MO. Additionally, it should be noted that there is a prerequisite for the production of MO, that is, learners have to notice the NF and perceive it as corrective. Ortega and Long (1997) have assumed that NF can facilitate L2 development because it promotes the noticing and storage of new input, and highlights the cognitive comparison between the new and old structural descriptions. Therefore, it seems that NF may facilitate L2 development through promoting learners' noticing target language forms and pushing learners to modify their previous output. The following sections focus on output and learners' internal capacities.

2.4 Output and SLA

The crucial consideration in any study of SLA is an understanding of the nature of learner systems and how those learner systems come to be (Gass 1997: 134). The previous parts have provided an account of where learner systems may come about. It has been argued that the learner should be aware of a knowledge gap between input and their interlanguage system through interactions. Because of the widely accepted proposition that input alone is not sufficient for acquisition, SLA researchers have begun to have an eye on output, which is a third component that has been argued to be required for successful L2 development.

2.4.1 Output Hypothesis

In the 1980s, the word "output" was used to indicate the outcome, or product, of the language acquisition device. Output was synonymous with "what the learner has learned". There has been a shift in meaning from the 1980s until now from output being understood as a noun, a thing, a product to output being understood as a verb, an action, and a process (Swain 2007). Output as a process "may force the learner to move from semantic processing to syntactic processing" (Swain 1985: 249).

Swain has attempted to examine the lack of L2 development by immersion children even after years of academic study in that language. By studying children learning French in an immersion context, Swain has hypothesized that what is

2.4 Output and SLA

lacking in their development as NSs of French is the opportunity to use language productively as opposed to using language merely for comprehension. She has compared results of various aspects (e.g., grammatical, discourse, and sociolinguistic) between sixth-grade children in a French immersion setting and sixth-grade native French-speaking children. The immersion children's lacking in proficiency and productive use of French has led her to assign the crucial role of output to the L2 development (see Gass 1997: 138–139; Gass and Selinker 1993: 277, for a brief discussion of Swain's important study of immersion children French learning).

Accordingly, in contrast to comprehensible input (Krashen 1985), Swain (1985) has proposed the notion of comprehensible output or pushed output, which refers to the need for a learner to be "pushed toward the delivery of a message that is not only conveyed, but that is conveyed precisely, coherently, and appropriately" (p. 249). She also termed this the Output Hypothesis for SLA. Swain stated (1985: 249):

> ...producing the target language may be the trigger that forces the learner to pay attention to the means of expression needed in order to successfully convey his or her own intended meaning.

In the above statement, Swain emphasized the important role of producing output as a trigger for learners' noticing target language forms. In an extended version of the Output Hypothesis, Swain (1995: 128) claimed:

> ...output may stimulate learners to move from the semantic, open-ended, nondeterministic, strategic processing prevalent in comprehension to the complete grammatical processing needed for accurate production. Output, thus, would seem to have a potentially significant role in the development of syntax and morphology.

Swain (2007), in a presentation on the Output Hypothesis, proposed that:

> The Output Hypothesis claims that the act of producing language (speaking or writing) constitutes, under certain circumstances, part of the process of second language learning.

According to Swain, output is supposed to be connected with learners' internal capacity, noticing, in particular. As a trigger of noticing target language forms, output is able to guarantee learners' interlanguage development. Additionally, it is through production that learners are able to receive NF during conversational interactions (Gass 2003), which has been discussed in the previous section. Therefore, output is also an indispensable component in L2 development.

2.4.2 Functions of Output

On the basis of the Output Hypothesis, Swain (1995) has elaborated three functions of output in L2 learning. The first function is "the 'noticing/triggering' function or what might be referred to as its consciousness-raising role" (Swain 1995: 128). That is, language production may prompt L2 learners to notice a knowledge gap between the target language and their interlanguage. Through the activity of producing the target language, L2 learners may be aware what they need to acquire in the target language. The second function is "the hypothesis-testing function" (Swain 1995: 128). In other words, output is an opportunity for learners to see what is acceptable and what is not in the target language. The third function is "the metalinguistic function or what might be referred to as its 'reflective role'" (Swain 1995: 128). This function can also be called negotiation of form, which has been discussed in the previous section. Learners may receive feedback by way of reflection on the target language form through conversational interactions. Then learning is supposed to result consequently.

Moreover, Gass (1997) has addressed the question how output functions as a central role in the learning process. She has proposed "four possible ways in which output may provide learners with a forum for important language learning functions: (1) testing hypotheses about the structures and meanings of the target language; (2) receiving crucial feedback for the verification of these hypotheses; (3) developing automaticity in interlanguage production; and (4) forcing a shift from meaning-based processing of the second language to a syntactic mode" (Gass 1997: 139–140).

As for hypothesis testing, Gass's emphasis is on output in the negotiation sequence. According to Gass (1997) negotiation and feedback can make learners be aware that when they produce language they are entertaining simultaneously. In other words, using language productively may promote learners to think about language. Gass (1997) presented evidence from the two aspects: talking about the form and self-correction. From the aspect of talking about the form, Gass (1997) supported Swain's (1995) suggestion that learners should conduct testing hypotheses through the interaction. Swain (1995) found the evidence of talking about the form in the interaction between L2 learners participating in an immersion program in Canada. Through the interaction learners were able to come to a correct conclusion after an initially faulty hypothesis. From the aspect of self-correction, Gass (1997) also showed pieces of evidence. For instance, learners received corrective feedback through negotiation sequences and were ready to fish for the right form (Gass and Varonis 1989). CRs could elicit learners' MO and learners could "test hypotheses about the second language, experiment with new structures and forms, and expand and exploit their interlanguage resources in creative ways" (Pica et al. 1989: 64).

As for feedback, Gass (1997) has argued that because feedback focuses on incorrect forms, it serves as a catalyst for change. When learners are informed of incorrect forms, they are likely to search for additional input for correction. If additional input is not available, learners can not obtain confirmatory or disconfirmatory evidence (Gass 1997). It seems that acquisition requires both negative evidence and positive evidence. Recasts, for instance, as a type of NF can also provide learners with positive evidence. The role of recasts has been confirmed by a number of studies reviewed in Sect. 2.3. However, recasts have also been found inefficient to elicit learners' modification. Pica et al. (1989), focusing on different types of NS signals to NNS errors, have found that the greatest amount of modification comes in response to CRs, with the interactional episode from Nobuyoshi and Ellis's (1993) study as an example shown in (7) below.

(7) NNS: He pass his house.
    NS: Sorry?
    NNS: He passed, he passed, ah, his sign.

Although studies provided evidence to support the role of feedback to a faulty hypothesis, Gass (1997: 147) has discussed the obvious limitations to this view as well. First, corrections can not occur with all incorrect forms. Second, many so-called errors are errors of interpretation for which there may be no evidence that an error has even occurred. Third, error acknowledgement, such as expressions of non-understanding (e.g., huh?), does not provide information that is sufficiently specific to inform learners where exactly an error has been made. It seems that the role of feedback has not been safely warranted yet so that more studies have to be done to deepen and extend our understanding of this view.

As for automaticity, Gass (1997: 148) viewed output as "the development of fluency and automaticity of processing" and demonstrated this function of output on the basis of the information processing account of SLA (McLaughlin 1987). With the assumption that the human mind has a limited capacity for processing information, McLaughlin (1987) has distinguished two processes: automatic processing and controlled processing. Automatic processing involves "a learned response that has been built up through the consistent mapping of the same input to the same pattern of activation over many trials", whereas controlled processing "is under attentional control of the subject and, since attention is required, only one such sequence can normally be controlled at a time without interference" (McLaughlin 1987: 134–135). Gass (1997) extended the notion of automaticity to output, and held that "the consistent and successful mapping (i.e., practice) of grammar to output results in automatic processing" (p. 148).

As for a shift from meaning-based to grammatically based processing, Swain (1985) has also presented the same view in the Output Hypothesis, that is, output "may force the learner to move from semantic processing to syntactic processing" (p. 249). Semantic processing is suggested to be insufficient in understanding the syntax of the language, which is essential to language production.

In sum, taken together, Swain's (1995) and Gass's (1997) further discussion of the function of output has indicated that output can "provide learners with the opportunity to produce language and gain feedback, which, by focusing learners' attention on certain local aspects of their speech, may lead them to notice either a mismatch between their speech and that of an interlocutor (particularly if as part of the feedback a linguistic model is provided) or a deficiency in their output" (Gass 1997: 148). Additionally, it seems that attention has played a role in the whole process in which output works. This leads to a discussion on learners' internal capacity in Sect. 2.5.

2.4.3 Psycholinguistic Basis of the Output Hypothesis

The specific functions of output have been investigated by many researchers (e.g. Ellis and He 1999; Nobuyoshi and Ellis 1993 for the hypothesis-testing function; Swain 1995, 1998 for the metalinguistic function; Izumi 2002, Swain and Lapkin 1995 for the noticing function). Despite the empirical research, what should be noted is the psycholinguistic basis of the Output Hypothesis. Izumi (2003) has elucidated the mechanism by which output may promote SLA by drawing on a speech production model developed by Levelt (1989; Levelt et al. 1999), the most influential psycholinguistic model of speech production. Originally developed to account for the speech production by L1 adults, Levelt's speech production model has been adapted to elucidate L2 learning in recent years (e.g., Bygate 2001; de Bot et al. 1997; Kormos 1999). A brief introduction of the model is presented below.

Levelt's production model consists of five distinct components: the conceptualizer, the formulator, the articulator, the audition, and the speech comprehension system. The model involves three sources of knowledge as well: lemmas and forms contained in the lexicon and discourse model, situation and encyclopedic knowledge connected to the conceptualizer, seen in Fig. 2.1.

According to the above Figure, an overt speech starts from preverbal message generation in the conceptualizer. Then the preverbal message is converted into a phonetic plan in the formulator through the grammatical encoding and the phonological encoding. Both the semantic specification provided in lemmas and the morpho-phonological information stored in the forms, contribute respectively to the grammatical encoding and the phonological encoding. Meanwhile, the phonetic plan is internally scanned by the speaker through the speech-comprehension system. After the phonetic plan is converted into actual speech by the articulator, the overt speech is then guided through the audition into the speech-comprehension system which is responsible for checking the output. In succession, the output is converted into parsed speech as a phonological, semantic, morphological and syntactic representation of the input speech. It should be noted that the conceptualiazer also functions as a monitor to attend to the output deriving from the speech-comprehension system either prior to articulation or subsequent to articulation (see Izumi 2003: 181–182, for a brief description of Levelt's model).

Production processing is not language learning per se, but "a process in which a concept is encoded in a speech form that is to be communicated" (Izumi 2003: 183). Likewise Levelt's production model is not developed to account for language learning. It can nevertheless shed light on how learning takes place through production processes (de Bot et al. 1997; Kormos 1999). As shown in Fig. 2.1, Levelt's model demonstrates how a surface structure of a message is derived through grammatical encoding which requires a focus on the syntactic form provided by the language producer. During production processes, grammatical encoding is requisite in message generation and formulation. Alternatively, production cannot take place without syntactic operations. In this sense, output can force the learner to move from "the semantic processing prevalent in

2.4 Output and SLA

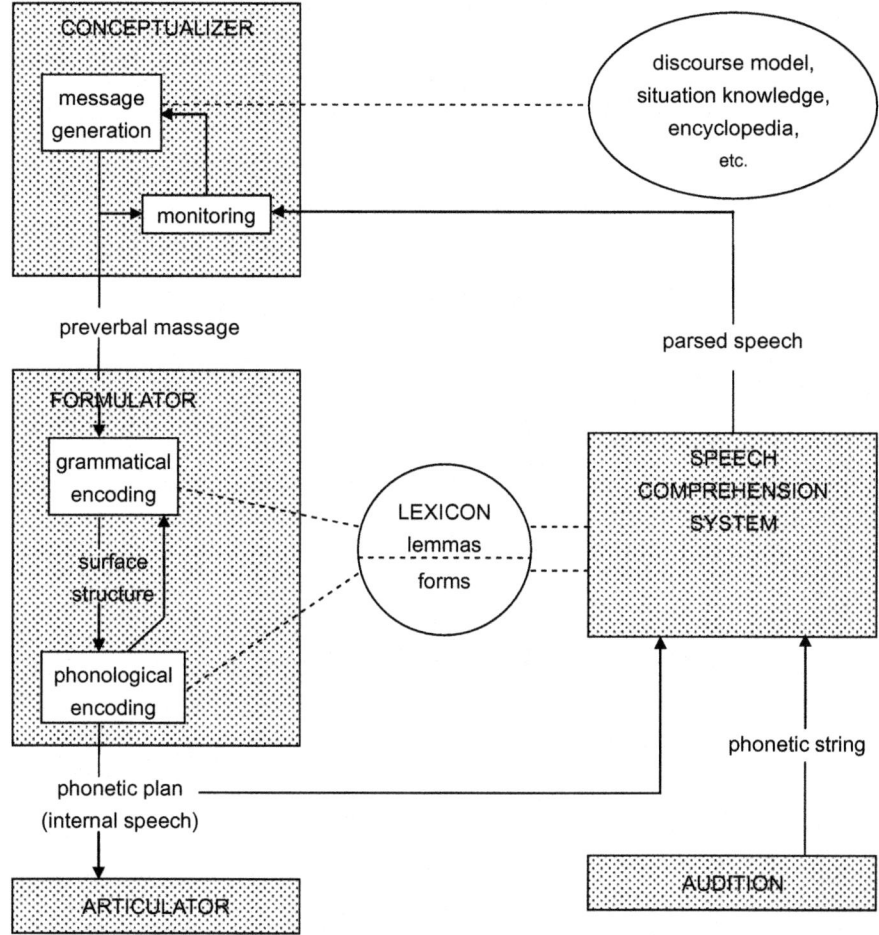

Fig. 2.1 Levelt's speech production model (Levelt 1989: 9)

comprehension to the syntactic processing needed for production" (Swain and Lapkin 1995: 375).

During the production processing, grammatical encoding and monitoring are regarded as the most important for L2 learners (Izumi 2003). Different from adult NSs, L2 learners require a great deal of controlled processing and attention (Kormos 1999). It is suggested that "the very process of grammatical encoding in production sensitizes learners to the possibilities and limitations of what they can or cannot express in the target language" (Izumi 2003: 183). Moreover, it is monitoring speech that supports such sensitization. As aforementioned, the monitoring mechanism is responsible for matching between the preverbal message and the outcome of the formulation and articulation. Thus, the monitoring mechanism may direct attention to the well-formed structures and appropriate expressions of the production outcome (Kormos 1999). Therefore, the production processes, in particular, grammatical encoding and monitoring, "can, under certain circumstances, serve as an internal priming device for grammatical consciousness raising for the language learners (Izumi 2003: 184). It should be noted that the discussion of input, interaction, and output in this chapter has all mentioned learners' internal mechanisms, particularly, attention which has been addressed in the following section.

2.5 Learners' Internal Mechanisms and SLA

Up to now, I have demonstrated that input, interaction, and output can all contribute to L2 development. However, none of them can work without the operation of learners' internal mechanisms, especially attention which concerns why a learner selects certain stimuli and ignores others and what role attention plays in L2 development. Additionally, having selected stimuli for attention, how do learners perceive them? This question concerns another cognitive mechanism, i.e., perception. Therefore, I will discuss learners' internal mechanisms of attention and perception in this section.

2.5.1 Attention and SLA

Researchers in the field of SLA have become increasingly interested in the concept of attention since the 1980s. The concept of attention has become especially important because of its crucial role in many aspects of SLA theory such as input, processing, development, variation, and instruction (Al-Hejin 2004). A number of researchers have pointed to the confusion regarding the exact notion of attention (e.g. Hwang 1999; Truscott 1998). Thus, I will first address the concept of attention and its related notions.

2.5.1.1 Concept of Attention and Related Notions

Attention has been a major concern in the research of psychology for a long time, but it is far from being dealt with explicitly enough in SLA (Schachter 1998). There are several related notions of attention with overlapping meanings in literature, such as noticing, awareness, and consciousness, often used interchangeably in literature. This may be due to not only the inherent subjectivity in defining these concepts, but also the fact that these concepts are inherently connected, with one often entailing the other (Al-Hejin 2004). Attention has been explored in the field of SLA in recent years, although there has been controversy over the definitions and operationalization of attentional constructs such as noticing and awareness, and their roles in L2 development (Mackey et al. 2002). In general terms, there are two major

2.5 Learners' Internal Mechanisms and SLA

theoretical positions on attention in the field of SLA: one put forth by Tomlin and Villa (1994) and the other by Schmidt (1990, 1993, 1995) and Robinson (1995, 2003).

On the one hand, Tomlin and Villa's (1994) study has viewed attention as a limited-capacity system and has supported a need to address a fine-grained analysis of attention which incorporates three principal components, i.e., alertness, orientation and detection. Alertness refers to "an overall, general readiness to deal with incoming stimuli or data" (Tomlin and Villa 1994: 190). Orientation refers to the idea that "the specific aligning of attention (orienting) on a stimulus has facilitative or inhibitory consequences for further processing depending on whether information occurs as expected or not as expected (ibid.: 191). Detection, as "the cognitive registration of sensory stimuli", "is the process that selects, or engages, a particular and specific bit of information" (ibid.: 192). In Tomlin and Villa's (1994) view, detection is indispensable for learning while neither awareness nor alertness nor orientation is required for detection to occur. In other words, none of the three components of attention require awareness, either to operate or as the result of processing. Within SLA literature, noticing is often discussed as a related notion of attention. Tomlin and Villa (1994) have defined noticing very concisely as detection within selective attention, not necessarily involving awareness. They have differentiated between detection with and without awareness, and have proposed "registration" rather than "noticing" as a more neutral word "for the cases that do not implicate awareness or for processing of nontargets" (Tomlin and Villa 1994: 200).

On the other hand, Schmidt (1990, 1993, 1995) and Robinson (1995, 2003) have argued for a critical role of awareness in learning. Schmidt (1994a) has identified four dimensions of the concept of consciousness, i.e., intention, attention, awareness, and control. Intention refers to the deliberateness on the part of learners to attend to the stimulus. Attention refers to the detection of a stimulus. Awareness refers to the learner's knowledge or subjective experience that he/she is detecting a stimulus. Control refers to the extent to which the language learners' output is controlled, requiring considerable mental processing effort, or spontaneous, requiring little mental processing effort (see Al-Hejin 2004, for a description of Schmidt's illustration about four dimensions of the concept of consciousness). Within the SLA field both Schmidt (1990, 1993, 1994a, b, 1995) and Robinson (1995, 2003) have described noticing as cognitive registration. In contrast with Tomlin and Villa (1994), they distinguished detection from noticing on the basis of awareness (Mackey et al. 2002). Schmidt (1994b) defined it as the "registration [detection] of the occurrence of a stimulus event in conscious awareness and subsequent storage in long term memory ..." (p. 179). Additionally, Robinson (1995) defined noticing as "detection with awareness and rehearsal in short-term memory ... necessary to learning and the subsequent encoding in long-term memory" (P. 318). Accordingly, Al-Hejin (2004) has claimed that Schmidt's and Robinson's definition of noticing may be represented as follows: noticing = detection + awareness. He has forwardly suggested that since it is impossible to be aware of something without detecting it, the equation might as well be simplified to noticing = awareness. Furthermore,

Schmidt (1993) has differentiated the two levels of awareness: awareness at the level of noticing (e.g., simply being aware of linguistic forms in input) and awareness at the level of understanding (e.g., understanding the underlying rules of the linguistic form). It is awareness at the level of noticing that Schmidt has claimed is crucial for language learning, whereas awareness at the level of understanding is facilitative but not necessary for SLA (Schmidt 1993).

Obviously, both of the theoretical positions presented above agree that attention is necessary for learning, whereas they have proposed opposing views on the role of awareness in learning, that is, a distinction between detection of input with awareness (Schmidt 1990, 1993, 1994a, b, 1995; Robinson 1995, 2003) and detection of input without awareness (Tomlin and Villa 1994). In this book, we have employed Robinson and Schmidt's descriptions of noticing which have been widely utilized in SLA literature, focusing on learners' noticing of the target language form in the context of interaction, in the sense of detection with awareness. Accordingly, attention and noticing have been utilized interchangeably in this book.

2.5.1.2 Role of Attention/Noticing in SLA

Although disagreement exists as to the amount and type of attention needed for learning to take place, there is a general agreement on the importance of attention. As stated previously, current SLA research has gone beyond general interest in comprehensible input (Krashen 1985), which is considered necessary but insufficient for L2 learning (Ellis 1994; Gass 1997; Long 1996). Instead, researchers intend to obtain a more precise understanding of how learners process, and interact with input to develop their interlanguage system. Given that not all of the input that learners are exposed to can be converted into intake for L2 learning, research in cognitive psychology and SLA has examined the role of attention in mediating input and learning (Izumi 2002). As Long (1996) has stated, attention may be at the heart of the Interaction Hypothesis. Negotiation and other types of corrective interaction can draw learners' attention to the parts of their language different from the target language. This may provide an explanation for the question how learners utilize the content of the negotiation to advance their own knowledge through interaction. Gass (1997: 132) has pointed out an important role of attention in her statement that "attention, accomplished in part through negotiation is one of the crucial mechanisms in this process". Attention may explain why interaction and learning are related, which has been suggested by numerous studies.

Meanwhile, noticing, as a related notion of attention, has been receiving an increasing amount of attention from SLA researchers (e.g., Ellis 1995; Robinson 1995; Schmidt 1990, 1994a; Swain 1985, 1995; Swain and Lapkin 1995). Schmidt (1990) has considered noticing as the subjective manifestation of attention which can be operationalized as a cognitive operation that takes place both during and immediately after exposure to the input. The significance of noticing for L2 learning has been proposed as the Noticing Hypothesis (Schmidt 1990, 1995, 2001; Schmidt and Frota 1986), claiming that "intake is that part of the input that the learner notices" (Schmidt 1990: 139). Thus, noticing is supposed to crucially require focal attention and awareness on the part of learners. The Noticing Hypothesis (Schmidt 1990, 1995) emphasizes the role of awareness in language learning and argues that learners must consciously notice linguistic input before it is converted into intake. Thus, noticing that has resulted in intake may lead to restructuring of the learner's interlanguage system.

Furthermore, the nature and the role of noticing have been refined. Schmidt (1995) has considered noticing as conscious registration of the occurrence of some event. Schmidt (2001) has claimed that noticing is used in a restricted sense with its object being "elements of the surface structure of utterances in the input—instances of language, rather than any abstract rules or principles of which such instances may be exemplars" (p. 5). In response to debate on the necessity of awareness in learning, Schmidt (2001) has suggested that the important question is not whether there exists any learning without involvement of attention and consciousness but whether more attention results in more language development. He added that "noticing is the first step in language building, not the end of the process" (Schmidt 2001: 31).

In addition, Robinson (1995, 2003) has agreed with Schmidt to the argument that no learning can occur without awareness at the level of noticing. Robinson (1995) identified noticing as "what is both detected and then further activated following the allocation of attentional resources from a central executive" (p. 297). He further addressed the role of noticing from the aspect of memory. In Robinson's view, learners are able to be consciously aware of the information when activation of information in short-term memory exceeds a certain threshold. Noticing refers to the "subset of detected information that receives focal attention, enters short-term, working memory, and is rehearsed" (Robinson 2003: 34). Accordingly, noticing is a consequence of this process of rehearsal, which makes it possible for that information in short-term memory to be encoded in long-term memory. In this sense, noticing is crucial for learning.

Finally, the role of noticing can also be addressed in terms of "noticing the gap" (Schmidt and Frota 1986), that is, learners may notice not only the target language form itself but also the difference between the target language and their own interlanguage. In order to convert input to intake, learners should make a comparison between what they have observed in the input and what they have acquired on the basis of their current interlanguage system. In most cases, learners are most likely to notice what they want to say but cannot say precisely when provided with input in the target language. Doughty and Williams (1998) have called this situation as noticing a hole in learners' interlanguage. Therefore, Swain and Lapkin have argued that noticing is in this sense crucial in L2 learning because noticing the hole may trigger cognitive processes that may generate new linguistic knowledge or consolidate the learners' existing knowledge.

To sum up, although there is still controversy on the necessity of noticing for SLA, the role of noticing for L2 learning has been investigated by a number of researchers (e.g. Adams 2003; Izumi 2002; Leow 2001, 2002; Mackey 2006c;

Swain and Lapkin 2002). In the context of interaction research, the relationship between noticing and learning is clearly warranted just as the Interaction Hypothesis claims that regular interaction works through learner-internal factors, such as noticing (Long 1996). However, theories of attention in SLA are far from being fully established. There is a need to further study what kind of interlanguage development results from noticing specific linguistic aspects.

2.5.2 Perception and SLA

Attending to the input is only part of the story because we need to interpret the selected information. This internal analysis of the selected information by the brain is termed perception which is closely connected with attention and contributes to human information-processing (Child 1981). Perception is also one of learners' internal mechanisms considered in the book.

2.5.2.1 Operationalization of Perception

Perception is originally a technical term in the field of psychology. However, in language acquisition studies, Saxon (1997) has used the term perception in a nontechnical sense in his Direct Contrast Hypothesis about the role of recasts in L1 acquisition: "…the child may perceive the adult form as being in contrast with the equivalent form. Cognizance of a relevant contrast can then form the basis for perceiving the adult form as correct alternative to the child form" (p. 155). This kind of nontechnical use of the term perception has also been adopted by researchers in interaction research (e.g., Carpenter et al. 2006; Mackey et al. 2000). Since we intend to search for the relationship between learners' perception and L2 development during the conversational interaction, we follow Carpenter et al. (2006), Mackey et al. (2000), and Saxon (1997) to address perception in a nontechnical sense. To term it another way, we focus on how learners interpret interactional feedback provided to them during the task-based interaction, and whether their interpretations of feedback may affect their L2 development.

2.5.2.2 Role of Perception in SLA

According to Long (1996), the linguistic modifications provided due to breakdowns in communication between L2 learners and their competent interlocutors may contribute especially to the development of learners' interlanguage system. The negotiation of meaning and recasts to accompany communication breakdowns are supposed to provide learners with NF and positive input in case of their problematic production (Carpenter et al. 2006). As aforementioned, the NF can facilitate L2 development in a certain degree when the gap between learners' interlanguage system and the target language is apparent to learners.

The NF in the form of recasts, for instance, has been found effective in promoting L2 development in numerous studies (e.g., Iwashita 2003; Han 2002; Nicholas et al. 2001). Nevertheless, some researchers have questioned the accessibility of the NF in the form of recasts given that recasts can be ambiguous to learners (e.g., Lyster 1998a, b; Lyster and Ranta 1997; Panova and Lyster 2002). The nature of the interaction may obscure the corrective nature of recasts and learners may fail to detect the difference between their deviant utterances and the corrective forms in recasts (Carpenter et al. 2006). In other words, when L2 learners have noticed interactional feedback provided to them during the interaction, they may or may not interpret feedback as intended, in particular, the NF in the form of recasts. As Long (1996) has stated, "from a learner's perspective, interlocutors might be repeating part of an utterance quizzically because they did not catch all of it, because the meaning was clear but surprising, because there is another way of saying the same thing, because they disagree, because something was linguistically awry, or for multiple reasons" (p. 433). Thus, learners' perceptions about recasts may affect the role of recasts in L2 development. As Carpenter et al. (2006) have suggested, a better understanding of how learners perceive NF during interaction is an important and necessary step in describing the relationship between interactional processes and L2 development. In this sense, learners' perceptions about NF may also be a learner-internal factor that affects L2 development.

2.6 Summary

In this section we make a summary of the theoretical framework mainly on the basis of the theoretical work done by Gass (1997, 2003), Long (1985, 1996), Swain (1985, 1993, 1995). According to Gass (1997, 2003) input, as a necessary but insufficient component in L2 development, is supposed to be able to facilitate L2 development when converted into intake, i.e., something meaningful as part of the process of grammar formation. Input alone is not beneficial enough for learners to develop their interlanguage system because one can interpret the meaning without the use of syntax. To compensate for the deficiency of input, output, as an indispensable component in L2 development, is claimed to have a potentially significant role in L2 development in terms of testing hypotheses about the structures and meanings of the target language, receiving crucial feedback for the verification of these hypotheses, developing automaticity in interlanguage production, and forcing a shift from meaning-based processing of L2 to a syntactic-based processing (Gass 1997, 2003). According to Long (1996), interaction, as a way to connect input and output, can facilitate L2 development by providing opportunities for learners to receive comprehensible input, to produce output, and to notice gaps between their interlanguage and the target language. As Long (1996) has also stated, the Interaction Hypothesis consists of some aspects of the Input Hypothesis (Krashen

1985) together with the Output Hypothesis (Swain 1985, 1993, 1995). During the interactional processes, learners' internal mechanisms, such as attention and its related notions, noticing, and perception, may also facilitate L2 development by attending to the target language form and being aware of corrective nature of interactional processes. Therefore, input, interaction, output, and learners' internal mechanisms function differently in the process of facilitating L2 development.

Based on such a theoretical framework the current study intends to make a deeper understanding of how interaction works to bring about positive effects on L2 development, which is assumed to be a result of providing NF conducted as input, producing MO in response to NF, noticing target language forms, and interpreting NF as corrective through interactional processes.

Chapter 3
Pespectives on Interaction Process in SLA

This chapter presents studies of different perspectives in interactional research. Section 3.1 is related with research on NF, consisting of studies on the effects of recasts and negotiation moves on L2 development. Section 3.2, then, concerns a review of research on MO, involving the evidence of learners' modification in response to NF, and claims of the effects that MO, particularly in response to recasts, has on L2 development. Following that, Sect. 3.3 presents research on learners' noticing of NF and perceptions about that feedback, recasts in particular. In succession, Sect. 3.4 presents a clear picture about research on English question formation. Finally Sect. 3.5 is a summary of the literature review and then points out the research gap in this field.

3.1 Perspectives on NF in SLA

From the 1980s, the growing body of research on NF has emphasized its importance in the field of SLA among the interaction-based research. NF has been investigated in regard to whether and how it promotes L2 development, NF in which form is more efficient to promote L2 development. Although no consensus has yet emerged from the diversity of research on NF, it does appear that NF, more often than not, plays a crucial role in L2 development, specifically in certain syntactic aspects. The following section is a review of research on NF and L2 development.

3.1.1 The Effects of Recasts in SLA

As described in Chap. 2, NF can take the form of recasts and negotiation moves, such as CRs, confirmation checks, repetitions, etc. There has been a growing interest in the role of NF, particularly recasts, in L2 development from the last decade. The review in this section begins with whether recasts promote L2 development, followed by how recasts promote L2 development.

3.1.1.1 Whether Recasts Promote L2 Development

A number of studies have supported the positive role of recasts in interlanguage development (e.g., Ortega and Long 1997; Long et al. 1998; Doughty and Varela 1998). Ortega and Long (1997) explored short-term effects of two types of feedback, that is, recasts (implicit forms of NF) and models (preemptive positive feedback) on L2 development for adult Spanish learners in the context of NNS-NS interaction. The target structures were direct object topicalization and adverb placement. The study did not conduct a delayed posttest so that the results obtained in the study might not reveal a long-term effect. Participants were found to be able to learn adverb placement, but were not found to be able to learn direct object topicalization. This result was due to the fact that direct object topicalization as the more difficult one of the two structures should be used depending on the context. The study obtained limited evidence for the argument that adults could be able to benefit from recasts in the short term.

Long et al. (1998) attempted to systematically demonstrate the role of recasts in SLA by conducting two studies to compare modeling with recasts, and to investigate the effects of correct models and recasts on the immediate development of Japanese and Spanish as foreign languages, with twenty-four adult learners of Japanese as participants in the Japanese study and thirty undergraduate volunteers from Spanish classes as participants in the Spanish study. Results of pre and posttests suggested that in the Spanish study, recasts were more effective than models in the acquisition of adverb placement, while it was not the case for object topicalization. As for the Japanese study, little evidence was obtained for development in any of the treatment groups. Although the findings were inconclusive, this study presented us the valuable finding that in a controlled environment in the laboratory recasts could promote adult language development in the context of NS-NNS interaction. Ortega and Long (1997) and Long et al. (1998) empirically drew a tentative conclusion that recasts were effective in promoting L2 development. However, they did not conduct a delayed posttest to examine the long-term effects. Therefore, their findings could not guarantee the maintenance of favorable effects of recasts.

A classroom-based study employing a delayed posttest in assessing the effects of recasts was conducted by Doughty and Varela (1998). It investigated the feasibility and effectiveness of incorporating recasts, as a relatively implicit FonF technique, into a content-based communicative ESL classroom, in which thirty-four middle school students as participants ranging in age from 11 to 14. The target structure in the study was past and conditional constructions. The findings revealed that learners who received the corrective recasts improved more in terms of developmental progress, accuracy, and frequency of use of past time reference than learners in a

3.1 Perspectives on NF in SLA   35

control group who did not receive systematic corrective feedback on both the immediate posttest and delayed posttest, conducted two months after treatment was provided. The study also indicated the feasibility of frequent recasting to facilitate ESL learners' interlanguage development. However, they suggested that these results awaited further investigation because "the repetition of the learners' error and the use of emphasis make these corrective recasts more explicit than simple conversational recasts" (p. 124).

Mackey and Philp (1998) have investigated the effect of negotiated interaction with recasts on L2 development between NS-NNS interaction in a laboratory context. They compared the effects of interaction, with and without recasts, on the development of question forms in English as a L2. Thirty-five adult ESL learners participated in the study and were divided into two groups. The less advanced learners received interactionally modified input through teacher-learner negotiation which could draw learners' attention to misunderstandings between input and output. The more advanced learners received the same input with intensive recasts. Results obtained from the pretest, posttest, and delayed posttest suggested that for more advanced learners, interaction with intensive recasts might be more beneficial than interaction alone in facilitating an increase in production of targeted higher-level morphosyntactic forms. In contrary, differential effects of recasts were not found according to the type of interaction in less advanced learners. Thus, the study suggested that learners would benefit from recasts when they were developmentally ready. The significance of the study lies in the fact that it has verified the benefits of recasts in a controlled laboratory context between adults NS-NNS interaction. In addition, this study has provided a suggestion that one of the conditions for learners to benefit from recasts should be the learners' developmental readiness to acquire the target forms.

Two domestic studies (Ni 2004; Lin 2006) explored the role of recasts in EFL development. Ni (2004) investigated the effects of recasts on EFL learners' past tense error correction. Forty-three junior students at two proficiency levels participated in the study, in which there were three treatment conditions, that is, recast, recast combined with metalinguistic, recast combined with explicit correction. The three treatment conditions were conducted respectively to the participants at two proficiency levels. The results showed that all the experimental groups scored better than the control group, and that two feedback combination groups performed better than the recasts group though no significant difference was found between the two feedback combination groups. The results also indicated that two feedback combination groups performed better than the recasts group for comparatively lower proficiency students whereas the recast combined with explicit correction group did not perform as well as the other two treatment groups for comparatively higher proficiency students. This study has suggested that it is necessary to examine recasts provided together with other types of feedback so as to better understand the effects of recasts on L2 development.

Lin (2006) conducted a study of the effects of recasts on Chinese EFL learners' output concerning subject-predicate agreement of the present simple tense of the third person singular. Thirty-eight first year college students were randomly divided into three treatment condition groups, i.e., the recast group, the non-recast group, and the control group. One immediate posttest and two delayed posttests were conducted to assess learners' target structure development. The findings showed that recasts had promoted the learners' use of the target structure in the recast group. The results indicated that recasts were a useful and effective corrective feedback for L2 development. However, the results obtained from both Ni's (2004) study and Lin's (2006) study may not be generalized for other structures. Thus, it is necessary to investigate the role of recasts in the development of other target structures.

The above studies have demonstrated that recasts can promote L2 development in a certain degree in the laboratory and the classroom settings. The use of delayed posttest is of great importance as a step forward to examine long-term effects of recasts on interlanguage development. However, some studies have questioned the effects of recasts in L2 development when comparing recasts with more explicit forms of feedback.

Investigated the effects of different types of NF on the adult ESL learners' learning of the dative alternation rule in English. They measured the effect of different treatments using the same items as in the treatment in the post-treatment recall test. Results showed significant differences between all the feedback groups and the control group. Results also indicated that the group receiving explicit metalinguistic feedback outperformed all the other groups, including the recast group. Additionally, only the group receiving explicit metalinguistic feedback maintained a long-term advantage.

Lyster (2004) carried out a comparative study to examine the differential effects of prompts and recasts in form-focused instruction in a fifth-grade classroom French immersion setting in Canada. Three treatment conditions (i.e., prompts, recasts, and no feedback) were implemented to 179 fifth-grade students by three immersion teachers in order to affect the learning of grammatical gender in French. A pretest, an immediate posttest, and a delayed posttest were designed to assess L2 development. The results showed significant improvement in written and oral tasks for all groups receiving form-focused instruction. Although differences among the three treatment groups were marginal in oral production, significant differences among groups were identified in written production. Results of written tasks indicated that prompts were more effective than recasts and no feedback condition. In other words, students receiving recasts or no feedback did not score as high as the prompts group. Thus, the study suggested that "learners who are prompted to retrieve more target-like forms are more likely to retrieve these forms during subsequent processing than learners merely hearing recasts of these forms" (Lyster 2004: 427). The results were interpreted in terms of the ambiguity created by recasts of gender errors and the difficulty for learners to notice recasts of morphosyntactic errors.

To sum up, despite the favorable effects of recasts shown in the above researches, recasts have been also found ineffective by Lyster (2004). It is necessary to conduct more extensive studies to corroborate the above findings, and to clarify on what conditions recasts can function as a facilitator of interlanguage development.

3.1.1.2 How Recasts Promote L2 Development

As aforementioned, recasts, as implicit NF, function by reformulating learners' immediately preceding deviant utterance with the corresponding target language forms. Accordingly, recasts, as an indicator of negative evidence, can also provide positive evidence to learners. Previous research has not determined whether the effect of recasts is due to their role as negative evidence or due to the fact that recasts consisting of positive evidence are more salient to the learners. Then researchers have begun to consider whether from the negative evidence or from the positive evidence the benefits of recasts stem.

Leeman (2000, 2003) investigated the specific benefits of implicit negative evidence and positive evidence provided by recasts through isolating independent features of feedback and input type through a laboratory experiment. Seventy-three students in first year Spanish courses participated in the study, randomly assigned to four treatment groups: (1) recast group (negative evidence and enhanced salience of positive evidence), (2) negative evidence group, (3) enhanced salience of positive evidence group, and (4) control group. The target structures were noun-adjective agreement and number agreement. A pre, post, and delayed posttest design was employed which took the form of oral picture-difference tasks. Results showed that only recast and enhanced salience groups performed significantly better than the control group in both the posttests and delayed posttests, while no benefit was found for simply indicating the occurrence of an error. Moreover, the recast group had similar effects together with the enhanced salience group. The results have suggested that at least enhanced salience of positive evidence could make recasts beneficial for interlanguage development, and that the implicit negative evidence may not be an important factor. The significance of Leeman's (2000, 2003) study lies in the finding that the benefits of recasts may derive from the enhanced salience of positive evidence provided in the recasts rather than the implicit negative evidence.

However, Ellis and Sheen (2006) have pointed out that it cannot be concluded from Leeman's (2000, 2003) study that all recasts work for acquisition because they afford positive evidence. In Leeman's (2000, 2003) study the corrective force of the recasts has been hidden. It is possible that if the recasts are more explicitly corrective they may constitute negative evidence and result in greater acquisition than the enhanced input (Ellis and Sheen 2006). Therefore, although Leeman (2000, 2003) has shown that the benefits of recasts stem from positive evidence, it cannot guarantee that this is the only way or even the most efficient way for recasts to promote L2 development. Given that if the corrective nature of recasts is made more explicit they would result in greater acquisition than the enhanced input (Ellis and Sheen 2006), it is necessary to reexamine the implicit corrective nature of recast.

The prevailing view in the recast literature regards recasts as implicit NF. However, implicit is vague in meaning, which has drawn researchers' attention. In Doughty and Varela's (1998) study, reviewed previously, corrective recasts contained clear signals to make the corrective force of the recast explicit. That is, the teacher repeated the students' erroneous utterance, stressing the deviant parts, and then reformulated the utterance, again stressing the corrected items. Although these recasts were didactic rather than communicative in nature, they were found to facilitate learners' interlanguage development. Subsequently Doughty (1999) proposed that recasts in L2 classrooms were effective when they were accompanied by some additional cues to make the learners be aware that the focus was on form (cited from Nicholas et al. 2001). Thus, in the classroom setting recasts seem to contribute more when their corrective nature is made more explicit.

Further evidence that recasts can benefit L2 development when their corrective nature is made explicit comes from Han's (2002) study of eight adult ESL learners who were randomly divided into a recast group and a non-recast group. The study adopted a pretest, posttest, and delayed posttest design, with eight pedagogical recast treatment sessions for the recast group and eight regular sessions for the non-recast group. The target structure in this study was the past tense. It was found that learners who had received the recasts were more likely to self-correct their past tense errors than a control group. The significance of the study lies in the fact that it "identified four conditions that may be necessary for recasts to facilitate learning: individualized attention, consistent focus, developmental readiness, and intensity" (Han 2002: 543). It should be noted that frequent, intensive recasts directed at a single structure encouraged the corrective nature of recasts to be explicit, which may promote L2 development.

Moreover, Ellis et al. (2006) study has provided evidence from the reversed point of view. They carried out a study of the effects of implicit and explicit corrective feedback on SLA with low-intermediate ESL learners as participants who were randomly assigned to two experimental groups and a control group. In this study, recasts were operated as the implicit corrective feedback, while metalinguistic explanation as the explicit corrective feedback. The target structure was English past tense. Statistical comparisons of the learners' performance in the posttests showed a clear advantage of metalinguistic information over recasts for both the delayed imitation and grammaticality judgment posttest (Ellis et al. 2006). The study demonstrated that explicit feedback was more effective than implicit feedback and contributed to the system as well as item learning. Notably, the results of the study also indicated that when corrective nature of recasts was not explicit enough, they might not promote learners' interlanguage development.

Additionally, an interesting case study was conducted by Nabei and Swain (2002). They explored the effects of recasts in a theme-based EFL classroom in relation to a learner's awareness. Although findings may not be applicable to other situations, they were still significant in making the complexity of recasts evident. Findings suggested that the salience and explicitness of recasts could be attributed to the intention of the recast provider rather than the linguistic elements, and that recasts occurring in communicatively meaningful interaction could have greater pedagogical effects. The findings also suggested that whether recasts were beneficial depended on learners, and that recalling the interactional episodes involving recasts was beneficial for learning. Nabei and Swain's (2002) study pointed to the importance of learners themselves in making use of recasts to the development of interlanguage.

To sum up, the above reviewed studies have shown the complicated nature of recasts, and have demonstrated how recasts may function as a facilitator in L2 development. More importantly, these studies bear out the claims of Nicholas et al. (2001) and Ellis and Sheen (2006) that recasts vary considerably per se in whether the corrective nature is implicit or explicit when investigated in different studies. However, the findings are far from being conclusive. Thus, more studies are needed to thoroughly explore how else recasts may contribute to L2 development. The following section makes a review about the comparison between recasts and negotiation moves in L2 development.

3.1.2 Recasts and Negotiation Moves in SLA

As stated above, NF takes the form of recasts and negotiation moves, a number of studies have examined the differences among these types of NF in various interactional contexts (Oliver 1995; Lin and Hedgcock 1996; Mackey et al. 1997; Oliver 1998; Lyster and Ranta 1997).

Oliver (1995) conducted a study to compare the utility of recasts and negotiation moves between child NNS/NS interactions. The eight NNSs were students enrolled in ESL classes and the NSs were enrolled in regular mainstream classes. It was found that child NSs provided recasts and negotiation moves (e.g., CRs and confirmation checks) in response to 61% of NNSs' errors when carrying out communicative tasks. Recasts were most often provided in response to utterances with a single error, whereas negotiation moves in response to utterances with multiple errors. Results also indicated that the type of interaction and their interlocutor could affect learners' opportunity for modification. The finding that discourse constraints and their interlocutors could affect the ways in which NNSs respond to various feedback types led researchers to assume that one kind of feedback is more effective than the others. However, Oliver's (1995) study did not assess the effect of recasts and negotiation moves on L2 development.

Lin and Hedgcock (1996) examined the provision and the use of recasts and negotiation moves among L1 Chinese speakers acquiring L2 Spanish in Spain who were divided into a low proficiency group (N = 8) and a higher proficiency group (N = 6). The results showed that both groups received recasts, clarification and confirmation, but the higher proficiency group was more likely to respond to the NF in subsequent turns than the low proficiency group. This indicated that participants were not able to notice or incorporate feedback due to their low proficiency, along with low motivation. Thus the study suggested that proficiency may affect NNSs' ability to modify their output in response to NSs' feedback. Like Oliver (1995), Lin and Hedgcock (1996) did not measure the role of NF in L2 development.

Mackey et al. (1997) also investigated the provision and the use of recasts and negotiation moves in NNS-NNS interactions with adult and child ESL learners as participants. The results indicated that both adults and children provided negotiation moves more frequently than recasts but children provided more recasts than adults. Similarly, Oliver (1998) compared recasts and negotiation moves respectively between adult and child NNS-NNS, NNS-NS, and NS-NS interactions. Like Oliver (1995), neither Mackey et al. (1997) nor Oliver (1998) utilized posttests to evaluate L2 development.

Lyster (1998b) and Lyster and Ranta (1997) explored the provision and use of recasts and negotiation moves in teacher-learner interaction in immersion classrooms. In Lyster and Ranta's (1997) study, there were five types of feedback taken into consideration: recasts, elicitation, metalinguistic feedback, CRs, and repetition. In response to learners' incorrect utterances, teachers responded 55% of the errors with recasts. The other types of responses occurred much less with elicitation 14%, CRs 11%, metalinguistic feedback 8%, explicit correction 7%, and repetition 5%. Results indicated that the recasts were most frequently used by teachers and were rarely followed by learner uptake as well. Lyster and Ranta concluded that recasts were not effective at eliciting student-generated repair compared with negotiation moves. This study has corroborated Swain (1995, 1998) in that negotiation of form techniques "push" learners to actively reprocess their output.

Utilizing the same database as Lyster and Ranta (1997), Lyster (1998b) has intended to investigate the relationship among the error type, feedback type and immediate learner repair. Error types included syntactic, lexical and phonological errors. Feedback types were recasts and negotiation of form (elicitation, meta-linguistic cue, CR and repetition). Results indicated a significant difference in the types of feedback that teachers used in response to different types of learner errors. Results also showed that in general terms learners' lexical errors led to teachers' negotiation of form while syntactic and phonological errors led to teachers' recasts. Additionally, recasts and explicit correction did not result in learners' immediate repair of syntactic and lexical errors as frequently as negotiation moves, whereas recasts encouraged phonological repairs. Accordingly, Lyster (1998b) suggested that for learners' syntactic errors teachers should provide negotiation moves to prompt learners to repair their utterance. Both Lyster (1998b) and Lyster and Ranta (1997) found that negotiation moves were more effective than recasts in eliciting learners' modification. However, they did not assess the effects of this modification on L2 development.

Oliver (2000) conducted a study to compare feedback types in response to child and adult ESL learners. She also found evidence for the provision and the use of NF, involving recasts and negotiation moves, i.e., confirmation checks and CRs, in both the adult and the child ESL classroom settings in response to approximately half of all nontarget-like utterances.

The studies reviewed above have compared the provision and utility of recasts and negotiation moves between NNS-NS, NNS-NNS, and teacher-learner

3.1 Perspectives on NF in SLA

interactions. It has been found in common that recasts and negotiation moves are provided and used in all interactional contexts, but different in the proportion of recasts and negotiation moves. Additionally, recasts are not as effective as negotiation moves in eliciting learners' modification. However, these studies have not assessed whether the difference between recasts and negotiation moves affect L2 development so that they are not able to show which type of NF is more effective for L2 development. In contrary, Iwashita (2003) not only employed pretest and posttests to assess the effects of implicit NF on L2 development but also found out the most effective type of NF for interlanguage development.

Iwashita (2003) conducted an investigation of NF and positive evidence in task-based interaction. The study examined the short-term effects of implicit NF and positive evidence on the acquisition of two Japanese structures. Fifty-five L2 learners of Japanese at the beginning level of proficiency in an Australian tertiary institution participated in the study. Results showed that, although NS's interactional moves containing positive evidence about the two target structure were 10 times more frequent during task-based language learning than those containing implicit NF, only those learners who had an above-average score in the pretest benefited from the positive evidence. Moreover, implicit NF was found to have significant effects on short-term development of the target structures. Additionally, recasts were also found to have a larger impact than other conversational moves (i.e. CRs and confirmation checks) on short-term L2 development (see Iwashita 2003: 1–2 for an introduction of the result).

In summary, the studies reviewed in this section, except for Iwashita (2003), have compared the provision and use of recasts and negotiation moves, and found out the ineffectiveness of recasts in eliciting learners' responses compared with negotiation moves, but they neither assessed the effect of learners' modification on L2 development nor found out the most effective feedback type for interlanguage development. Iwashita (2003) has verified not only the effects of implicit NF on L2 development but also the strongest effect of recasts on L2 development through the empirical study. Needless to say, the results await further investigation.

3.2 Perspectives on MO in SLA

In interaction-based studies, researchers are not only interested in the role of NF in L2 development, but also keen on learners' response to NF and its effects on L2 development. Numerous researchers have examined learners' modification (also called response or repair or uptake) in response to NF (Lyster 1998b; Lyster and Ranta 1997; Mackey et al. 1997; Oliver 1995; Pica 1988; Pica et al. 1989) and the relationship between MO and L2 development (Mackey and Philp 1998; Nabei and Swain 2002; Nobuyoshi and Ellis 1993).

3.2.1 MO in Response to NF

In the earliest studies of error treatment, some researchers suggested that pushing learners to produce output rather than presenting correct forms could contribute to their interlanguage development (e.g., Allwright 1975; Corder 1967; Hendrickson 1978; Vigil and Oller 1976). Later, van Lier (1988) argued that teachers should delay the use of corrective techniques because they "deny the speaker the opportunity to do self-repair, probably an important learning activity" (p. 211). Likewise, Chaudron (1988) claimed that the instruction encouraging self-repair was more likely to improve learners' ability to monitor their own target language speech. Additionally, Allwright and Bailey (1991) made a suggestion for teachers to allow learners in L2 classroom to do self-repair either self- or other-initiated. Calvé (1992) also advised that teachers should provide opportunities for learners to do peer-repair or self-repair (see Lyster 1998b: 184–185 for a brief review of studies of error treatment). These studies were all conducted through classroom observation. They all agreed upon the necessity for learners to repair their utterances through oral production.

In more recent interaction-based studies, MO in response to NF also aroused the interest of many researchers. Mackey et al. (1997) demonstrated learners' immediate use of implicit NF in the contexts of adult and child ESL learners' dyadic interaction. Oliver (1995) also indicated that the type of interaction and their interlocutors could affect learners' opportunity for modification.

Swain (1985) claimed that the provision of useful and consistent feedback and ample opportunities for output from teachers and peers might result in learners' production of MO which was necessary for L2 learning. Further, Swain (1995) argued that "modified, or reprocessed, output can be considered to represent the leading edge of a learner's interlanguage" (p. 131). Based on Swain's (1985, 1995) study, Pica (1988) and Pica et al. (1989) found that MO occurred most frequently on the condition that NSs signaled an explicit necessity for clarification rather than provided as recast for confirmation in a variety of dyadic interactional contexts.

Similar results were also obtained in the work of Lyster (1998b) and Lyster and Ranta (1997). As stated previously, Lyster and Ranta (1997) presented an analysis of interaction in four French immersion classrooms at the elementary level. Their findings reveal a tendency for teachers to use recasts, in spite of their apparent ineffectiveness in eliciting students' repairs. Moreover, the analysis of learners' uptake showed that 10% of recasts did not invite repair while 90% led to topic continuation. The analysis also indicated that teachers frequently utilized CRs not due to misunderstanding but for the purpose of drawing learners' attention to nontarget forms. Likewise, Lyster (1998b) found that recasts failed to inform learners of what was unacceptable in L2 for learners and suggested that recasts were not effective in leading to learners' immediate repair. Lyster's (1998b) study raised a noteworthy question whether learners' repairs in response to NF had effects on L2 development.

As Ellis (1995) claimed, "provision of negative evidence, especially, that which incorporates recasts ... does indeed facilitate the development of L2 syntactic ability" (p. 141). The significance of the above reviewed studies rests with the finding that MO is necessary for L2 development and CRs are more effective to elicit learners' modification than recasts. These studies, following Swain (1995, 1998), have indicated that negotiation moves are able to push learners to actively reprocess their output. However, these studies have failed to measure the effects of MO on L2 development with longitudinal assessment.

3.2.2 MO and L2 Development

Researchers have conducted various studies to explore the question whether MO promotes L2 development (Havranek 2002; Loewen 2005; Mackey and Philp 1998; McDonough 2005; McDonough and Mackey 2006; Nabei and Swain 2002; Nobuyoshi and Ellis 1993). Nobuyoshi and Ellis (1993) conducted an experimental study to examine the effects of MO and acquisition of past tense forms. Six learners participated in the study. The results showed that learners receiving CRs at least had short-term benefits for their acquisition of past tense forms. Although this study confirmed the effects of MO the results may not be safely warranted because the number of participants was too small.

Havranek (2002) investigated 207 EFL learners at different age and proficiency levels who were provided with 1700 instances of interactional feedback by teachers in the classroom. After the observation period, she implemented class-specific tests in order to elicit the learners' knowledge of the linguistic forms involved in the feedback. Then she found that learners were more likely to retrieve the linguistic forms that had been noticed with the direction of interactional feedback in a more overt way than the forms that had been recast. Nevertheless, the learners were more successful in retrieving recast forms that had been repeated immediately. The results suggested that the interactional feedback that led to learners' responses might have a greater impact on test performance than recasts. Therefore, the study demonstrated that recasts without learners' response might be the least effective type of interactional feedback. Havranek's (2002) study is an attempt to examine the MO in response to recasts and interlanguage development. The study indirectly indicated the positive effect of MO on L2 development.

Loewen's (2005) study is a direct example to show the positive effects of MO in response to recasts on L2 development in the classroom context. Loewen (2005) examined the effectiveness of the incidental focus on form, operationalized as providing recasts or metalingual explanation, in promoting L2 learning. Seventeen hours of naturally occurring, meaning-focused L2 classroom activities were observed in 12 different classes of young adults in a private language school in Auckland, New Zealand. The results showed that recasts facilitated learners' improvement of their linguistic accuracy while they were engaged in meaning-focused L2 classroom activities. More importantly, learners' successful uptake (MO in response to recasts) was found to be the best overall predictor of test performance. This suggested that it might be crucial for learners to produce the targeted linguistic items in MO during L2 learning. Additionally, Loewen also pointed out necessity for further research to explore the precise role of successful MO in the learning process.

Although some previously reviewed studies (e.g., Lyster 1998b; Lyster and Ranta 1997; Pica 1988; Pica et al. 1989) have suggested that the interactional feedback that can elicit learners' responses should have a more positive impact on learners' test performance than recasts which are ineffective to elicit responses, both Havranek' (2002) study and Loewen's (2005) study have revealed that learners may provide MO in response to recasts by repeating the targeted forms and that the response to recasts is associated with subsequent L2 learning. However, studies of Havranek (2002) and Loewen (2005) are based on classroom observation. Additional experimental research is still needed to investigate learners' MO in response to recasts and negotiation moves and to clarify the relationship between the MO and subsequent L2 development.

Some researchers have attempted to do such work. Besides the findings reviewed previously, Mackey and Philp (1998) examined MO in response to recasts which were operationalized as learners' immediate responses. The results showed that recasts had positive developmental effects for more advanced learners even though recasts were usually not repeated and rarely elicited MO from the learners. Accordingly, this study indicated that recasts could be beneficial for short term interlanguage development, even though they were not incorporated in learners' immediate responses. Moreover, the study demonstrated that learners' modification in response to recasts immediately after receiving such feedback was not indispensable for target language development. That is, it was found that learners' immediate responses to recasts were not significantly related to L2 development. Gass (2003) also doubted the effects of learners' immediate responses to recasts due to the possibility that learners might simply repeat the recast without comprehension.

McDonough and Mackey's (2006) study intended to gain a deeper understanding of the relationship among recasts, learners' responses to recasts, and subsequent L2 development. The study investigated the impact of recasts and different types of MO on the development of English question formation in the NNS/NS interactional context with fifty-eight Thai ESL learners as participants. In this study, learners' MO in response to recasts was classified into two types, i.e., learners' MO in the form of immediate repetitions and in the form of primed production (using the syntactic structure that was in the recasts a few turns later). Results showed that recasts were significantly predictive of ESL question development. Moreover, learners' modification in the form of primed production of the question forms targeted in the recasts was also a significant predictor of ESL question development, whereas modification in the form of immediate repetitions of recasts were not significantly related with question development. The significance of the study is to indicate that different types of responses to recasts have different effects on interlanguage development. Thus, additional studies are needed to examine learners' MO in response to recasts and L2 development.

Nabei and Swain (2002) have reported the opposite findings. As reviewed before, they carried out a case study to explore the effects of recasts in a theme-based EFL classroom in relation to a learner's awareness. On the effectiveness of recasts, results indicated that recasts provided opportunities for learning but whether learning could take place depended on the learner. In their view, if learners were aware of the corrective intention of recasts their immediate response to recasts may be helpful for them to acquire the target structures. Therefore, the effects of learners' immediate responses to recasts on L2 development should be further explored with learners' internal factors being taken into consideration.

Moreover, lack of modification does not assume recasts to be ineffective. As for the inefficiency of recasts in eliciting immediate responses, Gass and Varonis (1994), and Mackey (1999) suggested that recasts might have delayed effects on interlanguage development. In other words, the efficacy of recasts should not be neglected in spite of the possible absence of an overt oral response or modification in the next turn. Lightbown's (1998) study indicated that a response might be delayed beyond the next turn because learners were not cognitively or developmentally ready to produce an immediate response containing the recast form (McDonough and Mackey 2006). Oliver and Mackey (2003) pointed out that learners' immediate responses might be related with the setting and the context.

Additionally, a study conducted by McDonough (2005) focused on the effects of MO in response to NF alone and in combination on L2 development. McDonough (2005) attempted to identify whether both NF and learners' MO to that feedback were predictive of ESL question development. NF employed in this study was in the form of CRs and enhanced salience of nontarget-like forms. Sixty Thai EFL learners participated in a series of communicative tasks with NSs in four conditions according to different NF provided in the treatment period and different opportunities to modify output. A pretest/posttest design was utilized to assess ESL question development. The results indicated that the production of MO involving developmentally advanced question forms was the only significant predictor of ESL question development, whereas neither CRs nor enhanced salience of nontarget-like forms were significantly predictive of ESL question development. McDonough (2005) also pointed out a necessity for future research to identify whether both recasts and MO in response to recasts were significant predictors of L2 development.

To sum up, the studies (e.g., Lyster 1998b; Lyster and Ranta 1997; Pica 1988; Pica et al. 1989) have suggested that negotiation moves are more effective in eliciting learners' MO than recasts so negotiation moves seem to have more positive impact on L2 development. Thus, MO in response to negotiation moves is assumed to have positive effects on L2 development. Havranek (2002) and Loewen (2005) have indicated that learners may also provide MO in response to recasts by repeating the targeted forms, and that the response to recasts is associated with subsequent L2 learning as well. However, because these results are all based on classroom observation, they await further experimental verification. Then experimental studies have found diversity of results about the MO in response to recasts. Some researchers (Mackey and Philp 1998; McDonough and Mackey 2006) have claimed that learners' immediate responses to recasts are not significantly related to L2 development, while others (Nabei and Swain 2002) have supported the effects of learners' immediate responses to recasts on L2 development. Some researchers (Gass and Varonis 1994; Mackey 1999; Lightbown 1998) have considered that learners' immediate response to recasts is not necessary for recasts to take effect. Additionally, McDonough (2005) has focused on MO in response to NF alone and in combination and its effects on L2 development, and then has found that MO is the only significant predictor for L2 development. Therefore, additional studies are needed to clarify the relationship between MO in response to various types of NF and L2 development, and particularly to identify the effects of MO in different forms in response to recasts.

3.3 Perspectives on Learners' Internal Mechanisms in SLA

A number of studies have examined how interaction positively affects development, and one important line of investigation focuses on learner-internal variables. This section reviews research on learners' noticing and perception of NF in SLA.

3.3.1 Noticing in SLA

Attention, particularly noticing, one of the important foci of current interaction-based research has been investigated as a cognitive process that mediates input and L2 development through interaction (Gass and Varonis 1994; Long 1996; Mackey et al. 2000; Philp 2003; Robinson 1995, 2001, 2003).

3.3.1.1 Noticing and L2 Development

Previously reviewed research has shown that interaction containing recasts and negotiation moves can lead to L2 development. But how does it take place? Researchers have suggested that input should be internalized in some way to affect the acquisition process (Mackey 1999). According to Gass (1991, 1997), if learners are to make use of the possible benefits of interaction in which L2 data and feedback are provided, they must not only comprehend this L2 data but also notice the mismatch between the input and their own interlanguage system. As Gass (1991) stated, "nothing in the target language is available for intake into a language learner's existing system unless it is consciously noticed" (p. 136). Long (1996) purported the effects of selective attention mediated in L2 acquisition process through interaction. Schmidt and Frota (1986) emphasized the effects of noticing the gap, i.e., the interactional feedback could help to draw the learner's attention to a mismatch between their production and the NS's production. Schmidt (1990, 1993, 1995) claimed the effects of noticing for input to become intake. White (1991) also suggested that, for some target structures, it might be necessary for there to be incomprehensible input in order for learners to develop. Therefore, empirical research on noticing and L2 development has been strongly warranted.

In interaction-based research, researchers have tried to establish direct relationship between noticing and interlangauge development. Lyster (1998a, b), and Lyster and Ranta (1997) argued that recasts were less likely than other types of feedback to draw learners' attention to the language form in immersion classroom. Such results were due to the fact that in these studies, the noticing of recasts was operationalized as learners' uptake. However, uptake may not be appropriate as a noticing measure because in some conversational interactions there is no opportunity for learners to show uptake (e.g., Braidi 2002; Oliver 1995).

Egi (2002) investigated the effect of learners' noticing recasts on learning by adopting a pretest/posttest design. Twenty beginning learners participated in the study in which they received recasts of their nontarget-like relative clauses. The results showed that the group of learners with the noticing of 25% or more of recasts had significant development in production and recognition tests, while the group of learners with the noticing of less than 25% of recasts did not have significant development in either production or recognition tests. The results also indicated that the former group significantly outperformed the latter group in both production and recognition tests. Thus, this study verified the role of noticing in L2 development in a certain degree.

Then, Mackey (2006c) explored the relationships between feedback, ESL learners' noticing of the L2 form during classroom interactions and their subsequent L2 development in the classroom context. Twenty-eight ESL learners participated in the study. When they produced an error with question forms, plurals, and past tense forms they would be provided with interactional feedback, including recasts and negotiation moves. The learners' noticing was measured by a combination of learning journals, stimulated recall, and questionnaire responses. Results indicated that noticing was significantly correlated with both interactional feedback and ESL question development, but not with plural forms or past tense forms. The findings can be interpreted in terms of the different levels of communicative value of the three linguistic targets. Question forms may have higher communicative value than the other two items given that errors on question forms are more likely to result in a communication breakdown than errors on plurals and past tense (Egi 2004). Evidence that learners noticed interactional feedback would provide support for the connection between input, the learner's attentional resources, and intake. However, the study did not identify the effects of different feedback types on L2 development. It did not clarify the differences of noticing different types of feedback either.

On the one hand, the above studies support the direct relationship between the noticing of target structures and L2 development. On the other hand, McDonough (2005) reported an opposite finding. As previously reviewed, McDonough (2005) investigated the impact of NF and learners' MO on ESL question development. In the study the impact of reported noticing of question forms was also examined. Results showed that learners' reported noticing was not a significant predictor of ESL question development. However, McDonough suggested that noticing might have an indirect relationship with L2 development.

Up to date, the findings of the relationship between noticing and L2 development are not yet conclusive. Additional studies are needed to examine the learner's noticing of linguistic targets through specific type of interactional feedback and L2 development in order to have a better understanding of the role of attention in L2 development.

3.3.1.2 Factors to Affect the Noticing of Recasts

The learner's noticing of recasts is one of the focuses in research on noticing interactional feedback. It has been found that the noticing of recasts can be affected by many factors, of which learner factors and features of recasts are highlighted. As for learner factors, discussion is focused on the learner's target language developmental level (Mackey et al. 2002; Philp 2002) and on the issue of developmental readiness (Mackey 1999; Mackey and Philp 1998; Saxton 1997; Schmidt and Frota 1986).

Mackey et al. (2002) examined the individual differences in working memory capacities, their noticing of recasts and subsequent ESL question development. Thirty Japanese ESL learners participated in the study with a pretest/posttest design. All learners took an immediate posttest, and nineteen learners took a delayed posttest. Eleven learners were interviewed through stimulated recall which was used to assess whether learners had noticed question forms in recasts. Results indicated a complex relationship between the working memory capacity, noticing of question forms and the development of question formation. The relationship between learners' reports of noticing and their working memory capacity were marginally significant. The developmental level of the learner appeared to affect the relationship between the working memory capacity and their reports about noticing. Learners with high working memory capacities were more likely to benefit from interactional treatment after a time interval.

Philp (2003) examined the extent to which learners may notice recasts in the context of dyadic interaction. Thirty-three adult ESL learners were enrolled in the study in which noticing was measured by stimulated recall. The target structure was question formation. The findings showed that adult ESL learners whose level of question forms matched those provided in recasts would be more likely to notice the differences between recasts and their own utterances and would also be more likely to modify their previous utterances. The study suggested that recasts of question forms would be effective when learners' developmental level and feedback corresponded with each other.

Both Mackey et al. (2002) and Philp (2003) suggested that learners' interlanguage developmental level might be a factor affecting noticing of interactional feedback. On the issue of developmental readiness, Mackey (1999) and Mackey and Philp (1998) claimed that there might be a prime time in which recasts were effective in facilitating particular L2 forms, at least English question forms. That is, learners tended not to notice input beyond their acquisition level. Schmidt and Frota (1986) suggested that target forms might not be noticed until the learner was developmentally ready. Saxton (1997) explored the issue of developmental readiness in terms of the learners' prior knowledge and pointed out that the basis of a child's use and identification of recasts was his or her prior knowledge that two variant forms performed the identical grammatical function.

Then, the noticing of recasts can also be affected by features of recasts, i.e., length of recasts, and number of changes. As for length of recasts, Chaudron (1977), in a study of types of feedback in French immersion classes, suggested that recasts involving one segment of a learner's utterance led to more uptakes. In other words, shorter recasts were more salient for the learner. Lyster (1998a) reported the same finding in an investigation of discourse functions of recasts in French immersion classrooms. However, owing to the weakness of uptake as a noticing measure, the findings of Chaudron (1977) and Lyster (1998a) should be cautiously interpreted. Philp (2003) provided additional support for the salience of shorter recasts by utilizing stimulated recall. Results showed that learners recalled shorter recasts with greater accuracy than longer ones. This was interpreted in terms of learners' working memory capacity in which shorter recasts were more easily retained. As for the number of changes, Braidi (2002) investigated this issue in relation to NS's provision of recasts and learners' incorporation of recasts; Oliver (1995) investigated this issue in relation to NS's provision of recasts; Philp (2003) investigated this issue in relation to learners' noticing of recasts. Philp suggested that learners recalled recasts with only one or two changes more accurately than those involving three or more changes. In contrast, Braidi (2002) showed a tendency that NS recast more frequently in response to NNS's utterances with multiple errors (17%) than to those with a single error (14%), while no significant differences were found between NNS's responses to NS's recasts of single-error utterances and multiple-error utterances.

To sum up, the noticing of recasts can be affected by various learner internal and external factors. The review in this section is mainly related to learner internal factor and features of recasts. It should be noted that these factors should be taken into consideration in designing research and interpreting research findings.

3.3.2 Learners' Perception in SLA

The question how learners perceive interactional feedback, recasts in particular, has been considered by many researchers in interaction-based research. As aforementioned, some researchers have doubted the accessibility of the NF in the form of recasts on the grounds that recasts may be ambiguous to learners. Long (1996) claimed that recasts were ambiguous in that it was difficult for NNSs to decide "whether a NS response is a model of the correct way or just a different way of saying the same thing" (p. 449). Even when learners have noticed recasts, they may or may not interpret them as intended. It has been suggested that recasts might be interpreted as alternative ways of expressing the same meaning because the ambiguity of recasts might make their corrective nature hard to perceive (Braidi 2002; Egi 2007; Lyster 1998a; Lyster and Ranta 1997; Mackey et al. 2000; Morris and Tarone 2003; Nicholas et al. 2001; Panova and Lyster 2002).

Lyster (1998a) investigated the aspects of communicative classroom discourse that may affect recasts to be perceived as corrective by young L2 learners. The findings indicated that teachers' recasts in communicative classroom were ambiguous for learners and this ambiguity might restrict the development of target language accuracy in two ways, i.e., "(a) test hypotheses about the target language and (b) detect input-output mismatches with respect to form" (p. 75). Lyster (1998a) found that the ambiguity of recasts in classroom resulted from the fact that recasts and non-corrective repetitions co-occurred sharing the same pragmatic function. Likewise, Chaudron (1988) also stated, "the modification may be imperceptible, or perceived as merely an alternative to their own utterance, because accepting, approving, confirming repetitions occur frequently in the same contexts" (pp. 145–149).

Mackey et al. (2000) explored how learners perceived interactional feedback. Ten ESL learners received feedback concerning a range of morphosyntactic, lexical, and phonological forms. Learners' perception about interactional feedback was assessed through stimulated recall. In this study, morphosyntactic feedback was generally provided in the form of recasts, while phonological, lexical feedback was generally provided in the forms of negotiation and combination episodes. The results showed that lexical, semantic, and phonological feedback were relatively easy to be perceived as intended, whereas morphosyntactic feedback was generally not perceived as intended. Learners' failure to perceive morphosyntactic feedback as intended can be interpreted in terms of the ambiguity of recasts and the learner's limited processing capacity. This study has also pointed to a necessity to investigate whether learners' perceptions affect their subsequent L2 development.

Discussed previously, Philp (2003) also examined learners' perceptions about recasts. The results showed an overall high rate of noticing and pointed out three variables that constrained accurate recall, i.e., the developmental level of the learner, the length of the recasts, and the number of changes in the recasts. The study suggested that "the attentional resources and processing biases of the learner may modulate the extent to which learners 'noticed the gap' between their nontarget-like utterances and recasts" (p. 99).

Carpenter et al. (2006) examined learners' interpretations of recasts in interaction. Thirty-four ESL learners were engaged in the study. Among them, 14 ESL learners participated in verbal report protocol. The results indicated that learners who did not catch initial learner utterances were significantly less successful in distinguishing recasts from repetitions, and that learners did not tend to search for cues from their competent interlocutor. Additionally, morphosyntactic recasts were less accurately perceived than phonological or lexical recasts. This finding is consistent with Mackey et al. (2000). The study indicated that the contrast between a problematic utterance and a recast might help learners perceive recasts as corrective.

Egi (2007) investigated learners' interpretation of recasts that they noticed and the recast features that affected their interpretations. Forty-nine learners received recasts of morphosyntactic and lexical errors. The results indicated that when recasts were long and very different from learners' original utterances recasts were more likely to be perceived as responses to content, whereas when recasts were short and closely resembled the original utterances recasts were more likely to be perceived as corrective. The study suggested that length and number of changes might partially affect whether recasts were perceived as intended. This is consistent with the result of Philp (2003).

In summary, the research on learners' perception generally focuses on perceptions about recasts because recasts may be ambiguous to learners (Lyster 1998a; Lyster and Ranta 1997; Nicholas et al. 2001; Panova and Lyster 2002) Some researchers have also attempted to find in what conditions learners may be more likely to perceive recasts as corrective (Carpenter et al. 2006; Mackey et al. 2000; Philp 2003; Egi 2004, 2007). However, few studies have explored the effects of learners' perceptions about recasts on L2 development. Additional studies are needed to further explore the factors that may affect learners' perceptions about recasts as corrective and to find out the relationship between learners' perceptions of feedback and L2 development.

3.4 Perspectives on English Question Forms in Interaction-Based Research

The research on ESL question formation has been partially discussed in the previous sections. In this section we will put them together to present a more comprehensive picture of the current status of the studies on ESL question formation in interaction-based research. Among the research on English question formation, some studies have focused on NF and L2 development (Mackey 1999; Mackey and Oliver 2002; Mackey and Philp 1998; Spada and Lightbown 1993; White et al. 1991), some studies have focused on MO in response to NF and L2 development (McDonough 2005; McDonough and Mackey 2006), and some others have focused on learners internal factors in negotiated interaction (Mackey et al. 2002; Philp 2003).

White et al. (1991), in his study of ESL question development found that corrective feedback, input enhancement and instruction contributed to syntactic development. Although the study provided evidence for input enhancement to be able to present both positive and negative evidence, it did not illustrate how input enhancement was implemented.

Likewise, Spada and Lightbown (1993) also investigated the role of error correction and FonF instruction on ESL question development. Two treatment groups received corrective feedback with the target structure in FonF instruction, while a control group received regular teaching during a period of five months. However, because teachers in the control group also consistently corrected learners' various grammatical errors including question forms, the control group outperformed the treatment groups. Researchers considered that this result was also due to the fact that the control group was at a more advanced level of accuracy than the treatment groups.

As discussed previously, Mackey and Philp (1998) investigated the effect of negotiated interaction with recasts on ESL question development. Results showed that, for more advanced learners, interaction with intensive recasts would contribute more to learners' production of targeted higher-level morphosyntactic forms than interaction alone. Nevertheless, significant differences in learners' production were not found according to the type of interaction in less advanced learners. Therefore, the study has suggested that learners can benefit from recasts when they are developmentally ready. The study is also an indicator of a shift of focus in the research on NF and L2 development from whether NF, particularly recasts, benefits L2 development to how it benefits L2 development.

Mackey and Oliver (2002) investigated the effects of interactional feedback on children's ESL question development in a pretest-posttest design. Twenty-two child ESL learners, divided into two groups, participated in the study interacting in dyads with adult NSs. The experimental group (n = 11) were provided interactional feedback (i.e., recasts and negotiation moves) in response to the nontarget-like production of question forms, whereas the control group (n = 11) were not provided with feedback. Results indicated that the experimental group significantly outperformed the control group in question form development. Thus, this study corroborated the significant effects of interactional feedback on the development of question formation for child L2 learners. However, this study failed to identify which type of interactional feedback was more effective for ESL question development.

Mackey (1999) examined the relationship between various types of conversational interaction and the development of ESL question formation. The study adopted a pretest-posttest design with 34 adult ESL learners as participants who were divided into three experimental groups and one control group. Negotiation moves and recasts were provided to learners in the three experimental groups during task-based NNS-NS interactions. Results indicated that modifications in response to interactional feedback led to ESL question development and more active involvement in negotiated interaction led to greater development. The study suggested that "the nature of the interaction and the role of the learner are important factors, together with the type of structures that may be affected through interaction" (Mackey 1999: 583). Thus, Mackey pointed out two research lines, i.e., learners' modification in response to NF and learners' internal factors. However, this study did not identify the role of a specific type of interactional feedback in L2 development.

McDonough (2005), as discussed in the previous section, focused on learners' MO in response to NF in ESL question development. He explored whether both NF and learners' MO in response to that feedback were predictors of ESL question development. In this study NF took the form of CRs and enhanced salience of nontarget-like forms. The results indicated that learners' MO involving developmentally advanced question forms was the only significant predictor of ESL question development. McDonough also pointed out a necessity to examine the MO in response to recasts and L2 development.

McDonough and Mackey (2006) explored the relationship among recasts, learners' responses to recasts, and subsequent ESL question development. In this study, learners' MO in response to recasts took the form of immediate repetitions and primed production. The findings revealed that recasts and learners' MO in the form of primed production were significant predictors of ESL question development, whereas the MO in the form of immediate repetitions of recasts were not significantly related with ESL question development. The study suggested that learners' responses to recasts in different forms might have different effects on L2 development. Therefore, additional studies are needed to investigate various types of learners' MO in response to recasts and L2 development.

Then, focusing on learners' internal factors, Mackey et al.'s (2002) study showed a complicated relationship between working memory capacity, noticing of question forms and the development of question formation, which has been aforementioned in detail. As reviewed in the previous section, Philp (2003) centered on noticing and perceptions in the context of dyadic interaction. The results showed that learners did notice targeted forms involved in recasts. The results also indicated that adult ESL learners whose level of question forms matched those provided in recasts would be more likely to notice the differences between recasts and their own utterances, and would also be more likely to modify their previous utterances. Moreover, the study suggested that learners' attentional resources and perceptions about recasts could affect the extent to which learners noticed the gap between recasts and their nontarget-like utterances.

Few studies have investigated EFL question forms acquisition in domestic research except for Sun et al. (2007). They examined the effects of interactional feedback on Chinese primary school students' EFL question development in classroom context. 34 participants were divided into control group and experiment group. The interactional feedback provided for the experiment group was explicit correction and producing correct forms. Results indicated that the participants' EFL question development of the two groups was not significantly different with each other, and that interactional feedback could indeed promote the participants' EFL question development. The significance of the study is that it has shed light on the role of interactional feedback for the interlanguage development of primary school students in communicative classroom. However, whether this finding can be found for tertiary students still awaits further investigation.

To sum up, the research on English question formation has provided evidence for positive effects of NF and MO on L2 development. Researchers have begun to explore what types of learners' MO in response to recasts can promote L2 development and how NF, particularly recasts could be noticed and then perceived as corrective by learners through negotiated interaction. In domestic research, few studies have clarified how NF provided by more competent interlocutors, learners' MO in response to that feedback, and learners' internal mechanisms work together to promote EFL question development.

3.5 Summary

The review of previous research on NF, MO in response to that feedback, learners' noticing and perception about feedback has demonstrated the importance of input, output, and learners' internal mechanisms connected in interactional processes in facilitation of L2 development. According to the review, we can see that issues related with recasts are one of the most important focuses in the interactional research. Results on the effects of recasts, learners' responses to recasts, and learners' noticing and perceptions of recasts are still controversial and not yet conclusive.

Firstly, on the effects of recasts, a majority of classroom and laboratory studies have provided evidence to support the positive role of recasts in L2 development with various structures of English, Japanese, and Spanish as examples. However, in some other studies, recasts have also been found ineffective and ambiguous. Inconsistent findings may stem from different features of recasts employed by teachers or NNSs in different studies. Thus, it is necessary to clarify in what condition recasts can function as a facilitator of interlanguage development. It has indicated a change in interactional research to demonstrate how recasts promote L2 development instead of whether recasts promote L2 development. Moreover, quite a few studies have done some work on this issue and have shown the complicated nature of recasts. Controversy still exists in whether the corrective nature is implicit or explicit and whether recasts provide positive evidence or negative evidence or both. The findings are ambiguous and the issue needs further exploring.

Secondly, with regard to learners' responses to recasts, some descriptive studies show that recasts are not so effective in eliciting learners' MO as negotiation moves, particularly CRs and assume that negotiation moves accordingly seem to have more positive impact on L2 development. However, such assumption has not been verified through experimental studies. Moreover, some experimental studies have indicated that learners do produce MO in response to recasts either in the form of immediate repetition or primed production. The results differ in whether learners' MO in the form of immediate repetition has positive effects on L2 development. Therefore, the assumption and the contentious results suggest that more empirical studies are necessary in order to clarify the individual and combined effects of recasts and negotiation moves and to explore the effects of the MO in response to these recasts and negotiation moves.

Thirdly, on learners' noticing and perceptions of recasts, research discrepancy derives from the ambiguity of recasts. Recently many studies have focused on how learners can notice recasts and then perceive them as corrective. They have found various factors that may affect learners' noticing and perception, i.e., the

3.5 Summary

developmental level of the learner, the length of the recasts, the number of changes in the recasts, and the contrast between original utterances and recast. These findings are mainly related with two aspects, i.e., the learner and the recasts. Although some studies have established direct relationship, some have argued for an indirect relationship between learners' noticing of recasts and L2 development. Furthermore, few studies have examined the effects of learners' perceptions of recasts on L2 development. Thus, more work should be done to explore the relationship between learners' noticing and perceptions of recasts and subsequent L2 development.

In summary, built on previous research, the study of this book attempts to clarify what effects that NF, learners' MO in response to that feedback, learners' noticing and perception of target forms have on interlanguage development. NF in the present study is in the form of recasts and CRs because the former is still controversial in many aspects and the latter is shown to be able to elicit MO. English question formation will be chosen as the target structure in the present study because in domestic interactional research few studies have explored it as example to show the role of NF and MO in facilitating foreign language development, especially for adult learners.

Chapter 4
Issues in Research Methodology

This chapter is concerned with methodological issues of the present study. It starts by an introduction of objectives, research questions and hypotheses in Sect. 4.1. Section 4.2 presents a brief discussion on the operationalization of EFL development in this study. Section 4.3 amply illustrates how the study was designed, employing a pretest-treatment-posttest way to investigate the research questions. Section 4.4 presents the detailed information about the participants in the study, consisting of the EFL learners and the instructors as their interlocutors. Section 4.5 discusses a series of instruments designed and employed to measure a variety of variables and to assure the successful conduction of this study. Section 4.6 describes the procedures of the present study in detail, that is, how the research was conducted and how the data were collected step by step. Finally, Sect. 4.7 explains how the collected data were treated through data transcription, data categorization, data scoring, and data processing.

4.1 Objectives

The present study has drawn from previous research in SLA on interaction, NF, MO, attention, and perception. These areas are interrelated in exploring the research objectives, the effects of NF, learners' noticing target forms, their perception about NF, and their responses to NF on EFL development. By investigating how these factors affect FL development, the study aims to gain a better understanding of EFL development through interaction, to find whether both NF and MO are predictive of EFL development, to uncover which type of NF employed in the study has significant effects on EFL development, to explore the relationship between noticing and EFL development, and to identify the EFL learners' perception about feedback and its effects on EFL development.

Accordingly, the research questions motivating the present study are:

Question 1: What is the effect of NF on EFL development in the task-based oral interaction?

(1) What is the effect of recasts on EFL development in the task-based oral interaction?
(2) What is the effect of CRs on EFL development in the task-based oral interaction?
(3) Which type of NF can predict EFL development in a more effective way?

Question 2: What is the effect of MO produced in response to NF on EFL development in the task-based oral interaction?

(1) Do learners modify their output in response to NF on EFL development in the task-based oral interaction?
(2) To what extent does MO affect EFL development in the task-based oral interaction?

Question 3: What is the effect of noticing target form on EFL development in the task-based oral interaction?

(1) Do learners notice the target form in the task-based oral interaction?
(2) If they do what is the effect of noticing target form on EFL development in the task-based oral interaction?

Question 4: What is the effect of learners' perception about NF on EFL development?

(1) How do learners perceive NF employed in the study?
(2) Is there any relationship between learners' perception about NF and EFL development in the task-based oral interaction?
(3) What is it like if there is kind of relationship?

In accordance with the research objectives, it is generally hypothesized that in the task-based interaction (1) Instructors' NF has a significant effect on EFL development; (2) Noticing of target form has a significant effect on EFL development; (3) MO in response to NF is a significant predictor of EFL development; (4) Learners will show greater development when they perceive NF as corrective than when they perceive it as the instructor's response to content. In the next section the operationalization of EFL development will be discussed.

4.2 Operationalization of EFL Development

In this book EFL development was operationalized as question formation development, the dependent variable. The selection of question formation development has been motivated by both theoretical and practical reasons.

For theoretical consideration, the target form should be learnable by EFL learners through interaction in the study. Mackey and Philp (1998) claimed that learnability of one morphosyntactic structure was one of the factors to constrain its internalization by learners. Pienemann claimed that "the learnability of a structure was dependent on the readiness of the learner to acquire it" (Mackey and Philp 1998: 340). In other words, "... learners need to be developmentally ready in order to benefit from input, both positive and negative (Egi 2004: 116)". In addition, the developmental readiness of learners to acquire a target form may direct their noticing to the forms (e.g., Mackey and Oliver 2002; Philp 2003). Since all the related target linguistic elements about question formation had been taught before learners enrolled in college, they were readily to acquire various question forms of each developmental stage. In addition, learners may not acquire all types of question formation they were taught before, that is, their EFL question formation still needs developing.

Practically speaking, question forms were readily to be elicited through oral interaction according to many previous studies (e.g., Mackey 1999; Mackey and Philp 1998; McDonough 2005). Meanwhile, some researchers (e.g., Mackey 1999; Mackey and Philp 1998) pointed out that various question forms occurred at all stages of learning. Additionally, previous research (e.g., Mackey 1999; Mackey and Philp 1998; McDonough 2005; Pienemann et al. 1988) showed that the study of the developmental stages for question formation was relatively robust. Therefore, it was feasible to choose question formation as measure of EFL development.

In the book based on Pienemann and Johnston's developmental sequence for ESL question formation (Pienemann et al. 1988), the question development was operationalized as movement from one stage to a higher stage. This developmental sequence was also adapted by Spada and Lightbown (1993), Mackey (1999), Mackey and Philp (1998), McDonough (2005), etc. The developmental sequence for EFL question formation with examples in the present study was presented in Appendix C.

4.3 Research Design

A pretest + instruction-exposure + posttest research design has been employed in most SLA studies to identify the impact of such instruction or exposure on learners' subsequent processing of the second or foreign language data (Leow and Morgan-Short 2004). Accordingly, the present study employed a pretest-treatment-posttest design to examine the impact of NF, Chinese EFL learners' MO and perception on EFL question development. The tasks in the pretest, the treatment, and the posttests were all pair interaction between the EFL learners and the instructors as their interlocutors.

4.3.1 The Pretest

The pretest was employed to exclude the participants who were not qualified for the study from a pool of EFL learners. Namely, the pretest ensured that the research only included the learners who were classified at the same developmental stage of question development according to Pienemann and Johnston's developmental sequence for ESL question formation (Pienemann et al. 1988).

4.3.2 The Treatment

Since one of the independent variables under investigation—MO—was learner generated, it was impossible to order learners to produce MO or not. Therefore MO cannot be manipulated as an independent variable in treatment conditions. Instead, learners' opportunities to produce MO in response to NF can be affected in various treatment conditions. The treatment conditions were manipulated according to another independent variable under investigation—NF, in the forms of open-ended CRs and recasts. The two types of NF formed four kinds of combinations which represented the four treatment conditions with increasing likelihood for the learners to produce MO in response to NF. The four treatment conditions are described in the following section.

4.3.2.1 The First Treatment Condition

The first treatment condition was no feedback. The instructors did not provide any NF, neither CRs nor recasts, when the learners produced questions in nontarget language forms. The learners had no opportunities to modify their problematic output accordingly. The instructors had to maintain the communication even though they failed to understand the learners' words. An example of no feedback condition extracted from the present study is illustrated in (1).

(1) Learner 6: If the place is in school?
    Instructor: In the park.

4.3.2.2 The Second Treatment Condition

The second treatment condition was to provide recasts as NF. The instructors employed recasts in response to learners' questions in nontarget language forms. Immediately after the recasts, the instructors had to continue their talking without giving the learners an opportunity to respond to the recasts. That is, after recasts, the

4.3 Research Design

instructors answered learners' questions without any pause to ensure that the learners would focus on the answers in succession and not have a second thought about the recasts or modify their previous utterances. In this treatment condition, the learners had no opportunities to modify the output in response to NF in the form of recasts. An example of this treatment condition extracted from the present study is illustrated in (2).

(2) Learner 25: What place are the talk happen?
Instructor: Where did the talk happen? It's in a park.

4.3.2.3 The Third Treatment Condition

The third treatment condition was to provide CRs as NF. The instructors responded to learners' questions in nontarget language forms with the open-ended CRs. However, they were instructed not to provide any other feedback for the learners to have cognizance of their problematic utterances. Instead, the instructors had to make a pause after the CRs and provided the learners with opportunities to modify their previous utterances. In other words, in this treatment condition the learners had opportunities to modify their output in response to the NF in the form of CRs. An example of this treatment condition extracted from the present study is illustrated in (3).

(3) Learner 35: Why he is taking a photo for the woman?
Instructor: What?
Learner 35: Why is the man taking a photo for the woman?

4.3.2.4 The Fourth Treatment Condition

The last treatment condition was to provide recasts and then open-ended CRs as NF. Recasts were provided in order to draw the learners' attention to the gap between the instructors' utterance and their own. Immediately following the recasts, open-ended CRs were used to stimulate the learners to modify their previous utterance. After the CRs, the instructors paused to provide the learners with opportunities to modify their output. In that case, in this treatment condition the learners had enhanced opportunities to provide MO in response to the NF in the form of recasts and CRs. An example of this treatment condition extracted from the present study is illustrated in (4).

(4) Learner 51: Why they meet?
Instructor: Why did they meet? Pardon?
Learner 51: Why did they meet?

4.3.3 The Posttests

The posttests in the present study comprised an immediate posttest and a delayed posttest. The immediate posttest was designed to examine the impact of the treatment conditions on the learners' question formation development. Moreover, it was also targeted for gathering the information about the learners' perception of the NF employed in the treatment conditions. As for the delayed posttest, it aimed to identify whether the impact was sustainable.

4.4 Participants

4.4.1 The EFL Learners

It was assumed that the EFL question formation of the participants should get developed through treatment conditions in the present study. Therefore, the EFL participants belonged to lower-intermediate learners in order to identify the question formation development explicitly. They were 115 second-year students majoring in biological technology and garden design randomly chosen from a normal university in Jiangsu Province. Although all the participants had been taught English question formation structures in middle school, according to their present English teachers, they did not acquire all these structures. Thus, the participants still needed to advance to a higher stage in the developmental sequence for EFL question formation. Those who participated in the study would get corresponding scores helpful for them to be rewarded with scholarship. This assured the effective cooperation of the participants in the study. All of them were native speakers of Chinese, learning English as a foreign language. Three of them missed the pretest. In accordance with Pienemann and Johnston's developmental sequence for ESL question formation (Pienemann et al. 1988), of the other 112 students, 42 participants belonged to stage 3, 61 participants belonged to stage 4, and only 9 participants belonged to stage 5. Because the EFL question development of the majority of the participants was classified as stage 4, the final participant pool consisted of the 61 EFL learners in stage 4.

Data collected from the questionnaire of learners' background information (see Appendix E) showed the information about the 61 EFL participants themselves and their English learning. Of the 61 EFL learners, 40 were female and 21 male, 36 majored in biology technology and 25 in garden design. They were all native speakers of Chinese. All of them had completed their high school education before they were admitted to this university. Their ages ranged from 18 to 21 years, with an average of 20 years. The period of their English learning ranged from 6 to 12 years, with an average of 7 years. None of them had ever been in the countries where English was the native language except for one participant who had travelled in Singapore for a week. They seldom went to original English movies or read English magazines, and few of them browsed English websites on the Internet or watched English TV programs. That is, they had very limited exposure to English after class. It ensured that the participants' EFL question development would not be affected significantly by the factors not considered in the present study.

The 61 participants were randomly assigned into four groups. Group one (16 learners) was treated under the first condition, no feedback. This group was conducted as a control group. Group two (15 learners) was treated under the second condition, providing recasts as NF without an opportunity to modify output. Group three (15 learners) was treated under the third condition, providing CRs as NF with an opportunity to modify output. Group four (15 learners) was treated under the last condition, providing recasts and then open-ended CRs as NF with an enhanced opportunity to modify output. Each group was treated respectively under the corresponding condition three times.

4.4.2 The Instructors as Competent Interlocutors

The instructors as the learners' competent interlocutors in the present study included the researcher of the study and four experienced teachers of English with master's degree. The researcher then was a Ph.D. candidate in applied linguistics in the School of Foreign Languages in a key university in the southeast of China. She also had years of English teaching experience. The four professional teachers came from two universities where all of them were working as lecturers in the English department. Two of them were at the same university with the EFL learners. The other two were at a key university in the north of Jiangsu Province. They had never taught the participants before the study.

The instructors were informed of the purpose and the procedures of the present study. Moreover, they were trained how to complete the pair work with the EFL learners, that is, how to carry out the pretest and the posttests, how to do the treatment tasks in each treatment condition, and how to provide NF as required. On the other hand, they were also trained not to provide feedback to every question in nontarget language form in order to avoid learner irritation because of excessive feedback (McDonough 2005). During the pair-work interaction there were no fixed scripts for the instructors to repeat the conversation with each EFL learner. Instead they had to have cooperative communication with those learners. Additionally, the instructors were assigned at random to each group and were exchanged among groups so that the EFL learners would have opportunities to have interaction with different instructors during treatment sessions. All these conditions ensured that the instructors were qualified to manage the test and treatment sessions.

4.5 Instruments

In order to investigate the four research questions, a series of instruments were designed to measure the corresponding variables, and conducted to ensure the successful proceeding of the study.

4.5.1 Tasks Employed

The tasks in the study consisted of treatment tasks in the three treatment sessions and testing tasks in the pretest and the two posttests. The tasks were designed to create contexts for various question forms to be elicited, and to create opportunities for the above treatment conditions to take place. All the tasks used in this study were listed in Appendices A and B, in which the tasks were described by following the framework for classifying tasks put forward in Pica et al. (1993) (cited from McDonough 2005). They were employed and developed in many studies (e.g., Mackey 1999; Mackey and Philp 1998; McDonough 2005) with either children or adults as subjects. Thus, these tasks were apparently born with face validity. The materials of the tasks were adapted from some resource books (Smith and Arnold 1986; Ur 1988). The treatment tasks and the testing tasks are described respectively as below.

4.5.1.1 The Testing Tasks

The testing tasks, employed to measure the EFL learners' developmental stage of question formation, consisted of three communicative activities modeling on the tasks in McDonough's study (2005) but with thoroughly different contents (see Appendix A). Three sets of testing tasks were created for the pretest and the two posttests. Each set involved a warm-up activity (topic discussion) and two information-gap activities (preparing interviews and story completion) to elicit a variety of questions. The testing tasks were absolutely different from the treatment tasks for the sake of the reliability of the posttests. The three stories with pictures employed in the story completion task were extracted from Smith and Arnold (1986).

4.5.1.2 The Treatment Tasks

The treatment tasks, employed to treat the EFL learners with various conditions, involved information-exchange and information-gap activities to elicit various question types (see Appendix B). Three sets of treatment tasks were created for three-time-treatment. Each set of the treatment tasks comprised one information-exchange activity (picture differences) and two information-gap activities (story behind a picture and solving a mystery). The pictures employed in the treatment tasks were extracted from Ur (1986).

4.5.2 Measurement of Perception

The learners' perception about NF was measured by stimulated recall, one of the introspective methods. Gass and Mackey (2000: 17) noted that "stimulated recall methodology can be used to prompt participants to recall thoughts they had while performing a task or participating in an event". "Through the use of stimulated recall, a subject may be enabled to relive an original situation with great vividness and accuracy ⋯" (Gass and Mackey 2000: 17). Therefore it helps to elicit data from learners' statements about how to organize and comprehend information.

Stimulated recall is an important method for L2 research, for instance, in the oral interaction literature (e.g., Egi 2004; Long et al. 1998; Mackey et al. 2000). In addition, it is often used to explore issues on cognitive processes because these processes are usually unconscious (Gass and Mackey 2000). Learners' cognitive processes are difficult to be observed unless they are asked to describe the details during the processes. Stimulated recall procedures may provide useful data in the exploration of issues on cognitive processes (Gass and Mackey 2000). Therefore, perception, as a cognitive mechanism, is appropriate to be explored by the stimulated recall method.

When carrying out stimulated recall, the intervening time between the event and the recall and assistant stimuli should be considered for the sake of the reliability and the validity of this method. According to Gass and Mackey (2000: 18), "⋯ if the recalls were prompted a short period of time after the event (generally 48 h), recall was 95% accurate". That is, the method had better be operationalized as soon as possible after the event. On the other hand, a learner may recall details accurately "if he is presented with a large number of the cues or stimuli which occurred during the original situation" (Gass and Mackey 2000: 17). In other words, the stimulated recall method needs something functioning as stimuli to help learners reflect on their thoughts so as to explore their mental processes. Thus, stimulated recall should be "carried out with some degree of support, for example, providing learners with an audio-recording of themselves speaking, or giving them a picture they drew in response to L2 directives" (Gass and Mackey 2000: 25). In the present study, the scripts and recordings of the interactional episodes involving NF between the learners and their instructors were provided for the learners to recall their perceptions. Additionally, the learners' native language, Chinese, was employed in order to avoid any inconvenience for the learners' to recall their thoughts.

4.5.3 Measurement of Noticing

The study employed a learning journal (see Appendix D) to estimate whether the learners noticed question forms during treatment. The format of the learning journal modeled on the one used in McDonough's study (2005). The learning journal required the learners to write down any comments on what they had learned about pronunciation, vocabulary, grammar, and anything else in each interaction with instructors during the treatment. Any comment on questions found in a learner's learning journals was an indicator of his noticing question forms. Chinese and English were both permitted in writing comments. For instance, the comments written by a participant—在活动中我练习了如何提问，能够更顺畅的用英语提问—showed the evidence of noticing question forms.

4.5.4 Questionnaires Employed in the Study

There were two questionnaires designed to collect information from the participants in the present study. The questionnaires were edited in Chinese to avoid misunderstanding and to be timesaving. A number of distracter items were designed in the two questionnaires so as not to attract the EFL learners' attention to question forms.

Questionnaire 1 (see Appendix E) aimed to collect the background information of the participants. It consisted of twelve short questions about their natural background, their English learning background, their amount of English exposure outside classrooms, and their motives of English learning. Questionnaire1was designed with the reference to the study by McDonough (2005).

Questionnaire 2 (see Appendix F) was an exit questionnaire, intending to gather the information about whether the participants were affected by external influences. Those who received external influences during the period of the study would be excluded from data analysis. This questionnaire was designed with Egi (2004)'s study as reference. It involved two multiple-choice test items and four short answer questions concerning what the participants thought about the study and whether they received training on EFL question formation from other channels during the study.

4.6 Procedures

The experiment in the study was conducted over a 7-week period. The pretests were completed during week 1 and week 2; the three treatment sessions were completed in week 3; and the two posttests were respectively completed in week 4 and week 7.

4.6 Procedures

The stimulated recalls were conducted instantly after immediate posttests also in week 4. All the tasks in the present study were carried out through oral pair interaction between the EFL learners and the instructors in language laboratories. The materials and directions of each task were clearly printed out and distributed to each learner at the beginning of each test and treatment, while at the end of each test and treatment, the materials and directions were not permitted to be carried away by the learners. The instructions of each task were explained in Chinese to ensure each participant's precise understanding of the instructions. Each test and treatment lasted approximately 15 min. All the tests and treatment sessions were fully recorded by digital products for data analysis.

At the beginning of the pretests, the participants were required to sign a consent form (see Appendix G) which consisted of a general introduction of the study, the whole research processes, their signatures to pledge their cooperation in the study, and the signature of the researcher to pledge truthfulness of the contents in the form and confidentiality of the data collected during the study. During the treatment period, the 61 EFL learners, selected to participate in treatment and posttests, and the instructors carried out sets of treatment tasks three times. The instructors employed four different treatment conditions in communication with the corresponding group of learners. At the beginning of the first treatment the EFL learners filled out a background information questionnaire (Questionnaire 1). At the end of each treatment every learner was provided with a learning journal to write down what they had learned from this communication. The finished learning journals were kept by the researcher for data analysis. The immediate posttests were administrated after a short period of the last treatment not beyond the limit of 48 h. All the learners, except for those in group one, having finished the immediate posttest would go on with the stimulated recall instantly. After reading the instruction for stimulated recall (see Appendix H), the learners were provided with the scripts and recordings of the interactional episodes involving NF between themselves and the instructors in order to help them to recall their perceptions about NF during treatment sessions. The whole process of the stimulated recall was also recorded by digital products. Additionally, the learners' native language, Chinese, was employed during this period. Then two weeks later the delayed posttests were carried out. At the end of the delayed posttest the learners filled out an exit questionnaire (questionnaire 2). All 61 pieces of questionnaire 2 were gathered finally and they indicated that the participants did not receive any training on EFL question formation from other channels during the experiment. Thus, all the data can be used in data analysis. At the end of the experiments all the participants in the study were offered a gift for their whole-hearted cooperation.

Before the study, the effectiveness of the test and treatment tasks was assessed in a pilot study carried out among twelve Chinese EFL learners from a comparable population who came from the same university with the learners in the study majoring in biological technology. The results showed that the test and treatment tasks satisfactorily elicited various question types. Useful comments could be identified from the learning journals for the study. The scripts and recordings of the interactional episodes between the learners and the instructors helped learners to recall their perception about NF provided by the instructors.

4.7 Treatment of the Data

4.7.1 Data Transcription

All the tests, treatment and stimulated recalls were transcribed by the researcher and an instructor of the study. Of all the transcriptions, only the transcriptions of stimulated recalls were written in Chinese. The other transcriptions were all written in English. The researcher randomly chose 30% of the transcriptions from the tests and treatment data and checked the accuracy again. The inter-rater reliability, calculated with agreement of transcription rate, was 98%.

There were 234 pieces of test recordings, including all pretests and posttests, approximately 59 h. For the data from the test recordings, only utterances containing question forms were transcribed. Moreover, there was 183 pieces of treatment recordings, approximately 46 h.

For the data from the treatment sessions, only utterances containing interactional episodes with NF were transcribed. This kind of episodes in Group 2 started with the EFL learners turn containing at least a nontarget question form, and then was followed by the instructors' NF; while the NF episodes in Groups three and four ended with the EFL learners' responses to NF following the two steps of Group two. For instance, a NF episode extracted from Group 2 is presented below in (5):

(5) Learner 25: Why they come to this village?
Instructor: Why did they come to this village? Well, this girl was born in this village so each summer holiday she will come to this village to do something for local people.

The following is a NF episode extracted from Group 3:

(6) Learner 34: What is he often used?
Instructor: Pardon?
Learner 34: What is often used for?

Then a NF episode extracted from Group 4 is presented in (7):

(7) Learner 51: Why they meet?
Instructor: Why did they meet? Pardon?
Learner 51: Why did they meet?

Additionally, there were 45 pieces of stimulated recall recordings, approximately 11 h. For the data from stimulated recall recordings, only utterances containing the learners' perceptions about NF were transcribed.

4.7 Treatment of the Data

4.7.2 Data Categorization

4.7.2.1 Tests Data Categorization

The questions produced by the EFL learners in the pretest and two posttests were categorized to determine the developmental stage of each question, and to estimate the developmental stage for question forms of each participant in the present study. The developmental stage of each question was determined according to Pienemann and Johnston's developmental sequence for ESL question formation (Pienemann et al. 1988). As for the developmental stages for question forms of each participant, Pienemann and his colleagues supposed that "two different usages of two different structures are sufficient evidence that a stage has been acquired" (Mackey 1999: 567). The present study adopted a more conservative criterion that the question formation development was considered to occur when the EFL learners presented at least two examples of target structures in every task to elicit question forms in both the immediate posttest and the delayed posttest. In addition, following McDonough (2005: 88) a variety of question types were removed from the data. These question type included "incomplete questions, such as how about the man in the car?; echo questions; multiple exemplars of the same question on the same task; and formulaic chunks, such as do you like + object?". After the researcher and an instructor categorized all the tests data, the researcher randomly selected 30% of the test data to check the question stage categorization again. The inter-rater reliability, calculated with agreement of categorizing rate, was 97%.

4.7.2.2 Stimulated Recall Data Categorization

The learners' comments on each interactional episode in stimulated recall data were generally classified into five categories according to the transcriptions of the learners' comments. The five categories were: (1) the instructor was correcting my grammatical errors, such as "我当时觉得老师和我说的不同，是在纠正我犯的语法错误"; (2) the instructor did not understand what I said, such as "我当时觉得可能我说的太快了,老师没听懂我说的,所以就让我再说一遍"; (3) the instructor is helping me to finish the task, such as "我觉得老师说出了我不会的词,`能够让我继续问下一题"; (4) I did not notice what the instructor said, but was thinking how to continue the task, such as "我当时在猜想图片里哪里少了一个人, 所以没有注意老师说的什么"; (5) I did not remember the situation at that time, such as "对这段没什么印象了".

4.7.3 Data Scoring

Data in the study were scored by a binary system. If one of the following conditions was met it was scored as 1 point, including receiving a recast, receiving a CR, reporting noticing question forms, providing MO with question forms of stage 5, question formation developing into stage 5 based on the both posttests. Instead, the contrary conditions were scored as 0 point.

Since the EFL learners' question forms at the beginning of the study were at stage 4, only MO comprising stage 5 questions was regarded helpful for question development. Thus, the number of MO involving stage 5 questions was counted. Moreover, the number of NF provided in the treatment sessions, the number of learners reporting noticing question forms during the treatment sessions and the number of learners developing into stage 5 in question forms were also counted for data analysis.

As for the data collected by the stimulated recall, the learners' perception about NF was category-based. The number of each perception category of the learners in each treatment was counted for data analysis.

4.7.4 Data Processing

The data of the present study were processed by the analytical software SPSS (Statistical Package for the Social Sciences) 11.5. On the one hand, the data about NF, MO, attention and EFL question development were analyzed to answer research questions 1, 2, and 3, that is, the effects of NF, MO, and noticing target forms on EFL question development. On the other hand, the data about EFL learners' perceptions and question development were analyzed all together to answer research question 4, that is, learners' perceptions about NF and their effect on EFL question development.

Chapter 5
Effects of Interaction Process on EFL Development

This chapter presents and discusses the research findings in detail. Due to the different statistical methods employed in data analysis, the results of research questions 1, 2, and 3 have been presented together in Sect. 5.1, with the results of research question 4 being presented alone in Sect. 5.2. Section 5.1 investigates the effects of NF in the form of recasts and CRs, MO, and attention to question forms on EFL question development. Section 5.2 examines the learners' perception of NF employed in the present study, and its effects on EFL question development. Then Sect. 5.3 focuses on the discussion about the findings concerning each research question. In the discussion part, we not only explore what effects the NF in the form of recasts and CRs, MO, attention to question forms, and the learners' perceptions about the NF have on EFL development, but also try to elucidate how these factors affect EFL development. Additionally, in the discussion part we also concern the interrelationship among these factors during the interactional process.

5.1 Effects of Negative Feedback, Modified Output, Attention on EFL Development

As aforementioned in Chap. 4, a holistic analysis of the data about NF, MO, attention and EFL question development were conducted firstly to answer research questions 1, 2, and 3, that is, the effects of NF, MO, and noticing target forms on EFL question development.

5.1.1 Data Input in SPSS

After previous steps of data transcription, categorization, and scoring, the data were ready to be processed by SPSS. In the SPSS data set, the data were input in two ways, involving subject by subject and group by group.

When the data were input subject by subject, there were 10 variables: Group (treatment group), Number (number of subject), Sex (male = 1, female = 0), Recast (the subject was provided with recasts = 1, the subject was not provided with recasts = 0), CR (the subject was provided with CRs = 1, the subject was not provided with CRs = 0), reported attention (RA) (the subject reported attention to question forms = 1, the subject did not report attention to question forms = 0), MO (the number of MO involving stage 5 questions), question development in the immediate posttest (QD1) (the subject's question development moved to stage 5 in the immediate posttest = 1, the subject's question development did not move to stage 5 in the immediate posttest = 0), question development in the delayed posttest (QD2) (the subject's question development moved to stage 5 in the delayed posttest = 1, the subject's question development did not move to stage 5 in the delayed posttest = 0), and final judgment of question development in the experiment (QD) (the subject's question development was considered to move to stage 5 in the experiment = 1, the subject's question development was not considered to move to stage 5 in the experiment = 0). All the variables, except for Group, Number, and MO, were binary data. The extracted 30 subjects' data input in SPSS data set are shown in Fig. 5.1 as example.

When the data were input by group, there were 7 variables: Group (treatment group), NF (the number of NF provided in each group), MO (the number of MO involving stage 5 questions in each group), RA (the number of subjects who reported attention to question forms in each group), QD1 (the number of subjects in each group who developed to stage 5 in the developmental sequence of question formation in the immediate posttest), QD2 (the number of subjects in each group who developed into stage 5 in the delayed posttest), and QD (the number of subjects in each group who were finally considered to have developed to stage 5 in the experiment). The data input by group in SPSS data set are shown in Fig. 5.2.

5.1.2 Treatment Task Data Analysis

5.1.2.1 Data Description

As shown in Chap. 4, during the treatment sessions, the four groups of subjects were treated by four conditions respectively. Table 5.1 shows the subjects' performance of each group under various treatment conditions, consisting of the number of provided NF, the number of MO with stage 5 questions, the number of subjects who have made any comments on question forms in the learning journals, etc.

5.1 Effects of Negative Feedback, Modified Output, Attention on EFL Development

	group	number	sex	recast	cr	ra	mo	qd1	qd2	qd
1	1.00	1.00	1.00	.00	.00	.00	.00	.00	.00	.00
2	1.00	2.00	.00	.00	.00	1.00	.00	1.00	1.00	1.00
3	1.00	3.00	1.00	.00	.00	.00	.00	.00	.00	.00
4	1.00	4.00	.00	.00	.00	.00	.00	1.00	.00	.00
5	1.00	5.00	1.00	.00	.00	.00	.00	.00	.00	.00
6	1.00	6.00	.00	.00	.00	.00	.00	.00	.00	.00
7	1.00	7.00	1.00	.00	.00	.00	.00	.00	.00	.00
8	1.00	8.00	.00	.00	.00	.00	.00	.00	.00	.00
9	1.00	9.00	1.00	.00	.00	.00	.00	.00	1.00	.00
10	1.00	10.00	1.00	.00	.00	1.00	.00	.00	.00	.00
11	1.00	11.00	.00	.00	.00	.00	.00	.00	.00	.00
12	1.00	12.00	1.00	.00	.00	.00	.00	.00	.00	.00
13	1.00	13.00	.00	.00	.00	.00	.00	1.00	1.00	1.00
14	1.00	14.00	.00	.00	.00	1.00	.00	.00	.00	.00
15	1.00	15.00	.00	.00	.00	1.00	.00	.00	.00	.00
16	1.00	16.00	1.00	.00	.00	1.00	.00	.00	.00	.00
17	2.00	17.00	.00	1.00	.00	1.00	.00	.00	.00	.00
18	2.00	18.00	.00	1.00	.00	1.00	.00	.00	1.00	.00
19	2.00	19.00	.00	1.00	.00	1.00	.00	1.00	1.00	1.00
20	2.00	20.00	.00	1.00	.00	.00	.00	1.00	.00	.00
21	2.00	21.00	1.00	1.00	.00	.00	.00	.00	.00	.00
22	2.00	22.00	.00	1.00	.00	.00	.00	.00	.00	.00
23	2.00	23.00	.00	1.00	.00	.00	.00	1.00	.00	.00
24	2.00	24.00	1.00	1.00	.00	.00	.00	1.00	1.00	1.00
25	2.00	25.00	.00	1.00	.00	.00	.00	.00	.00	.00
26	2.00	26.00	1.00	1.00	.00	1.00	.00	1.00	.00	.00
27	2.00	27.00	.00	1.00	.00	.00	.00	.00	.00	.00
28	2.00	28.00	.00	1.00	.00	.00	.00	.00	.00	.00
29	2.00	29.00	.00	1.00	.00	1.00	.00	1.00	1.00	1.00
30	2.00	30.00	.00	1.00	.00	.00	.00	.00	.00	.00

Fig. 5.1 Example of SPSS data input subject by subject

	group	nf	mo	ra	qd1	qd2	qd
1	1.00	.00	.00	5.00	3.00	3.00	2.00
2	2.00	197.00	.00	6.00	6.00	4.00	3.00
3	3.00	154.00	13.00	6.00	7.00	8.00	5.00
4	4.00	156.00	36.00	10.00	11.00	10.00	9.00

Fig. 5.2 SPSS data input group by group

Table 5.1 Treatment task performance of each group

Group	Subjects	Treatment condition	NF	MO	Attention
1	16	No feedback	0	0	5
2	15	Recasts (no opportunity to modify)	197	0	6
3	15	CRs (with opportunity to modify)	154	13	6
4	15	Recasts + CRs (enhanced opportunity to modify)	156	36	10

According to Table 5.1, the first group of the subjects did not receive any NF, and consequently they did not produce any MO. But in this group there were still 5 subjects reporting attention to question forms. Although the second group of subjects received the most NF, they did not produce any MO because they were not given opportunities to do modification. In this group there were 6 subjects reporting attention to question forms. Both the third group and the fourth group of the subjects were given opportunities to modify their output when receiving NF. Moreover, the fourth group was provided with enhanced opportunities to do modification, where more subjects reported attention to question forms than the subjects in the third group. Hence, the fourth group of subjects provided MO consisting of more stage 5 questions than the third group.

5.1.2.2 Kruskal-Wallis Test and Mann-Whitney Test

Before the data are processed for later analysis, it is necessary to test the significance of the differences of the NF provided to the three groups and the MO produced by the two groups. Because the treatment task data were not normally distributed and the variance was not equal, the nonparametric statistics were employed to test the significance. Thus, a Kruskal-Wallis test was used to test the significance of the difference of the NF provided to the three groups. Additionally, a Mann-Whitney test was used to test the significance of the difference of the MO produced by the two groups where opportunities were given for the learners' to do modification. Tables 5.2 and 5.3 show the test results.

The Kruskal-Wallis test result in Table 5.2 indicates that the difference in the amount of NF provided to the three groups during the treatment sessions is not significant ($p = 0.368 > 0.05$). In addition, the Mann-Whitney test result in Table 5.3 indicates that the difference in the amount of MO produced by the two groups with opportunities to do modification is not significant ($p = 0.317 > 0.05$) either. Therefore, the differences of the NF provided to the three groups and the MO produced by the two groups may not affect the experiment results.

5.1.3 Test Data Analysis

As previously mentioned in Chap. 4, the posttests consisted of the immediate posttest and the delayed posttest. Only those subjects who advanced to stage 5 in both the posttests were considered to have developed in the developmental sequence of question formation. Accordingly, in order to identify the effects of each independent variable on EFL question development, this section has involved the

Table 5.2 Kruskal-Wallis test of the difference of the NF between groups[a]

	NF
Chi-square	2.000
df	2
Asymp. Sig.	0.368

[a]Grouping variable: GROUP

5.1 Effects of Negative Feedback, Modified Output, Attention on EFL Development

Table 5.3 Mann-Whitney test of the difference of the MO between groups[a]

	MO
Mann-Whitney U	0.000
Wilcoxon W	1.000
Z	−1.000
Asymp. Sig. (2-tailed)	0.317

[a]Grouping Variable: GROUP

data analysis on the basis of the final judgment of EFL question development and the subjects' question development in each posttest, respectively.

5.1.3.1 Data Description

Only those subjects who have met the requirements of stage 5 in both the posttests are considered to have actually advanced to stage 5 in the developmental sequence of question formation. The numbers of the subjects in each group having developed to stage 5 in the two posttests are calculated in Table 5.4.

As shown in Table 5.4, in the immediate posttest 11 of 15 subjects developed to stage 5 in the group with an enhanced opportunity, 7 of 15 subjects developed to stage 5 in the group with an opportunity to modify, and only 3 out of 16 subjects developed to stage 5 in no feedback group. In the delayed posttest, 10 of 15 subjects advanced to stage 5 in the group with an enhanced opportunity, 8 of 15 subjects advanced to stage 5 in the group with an opportunity to modify, and only 3 out of 16 subjects advanced to stage 5 in no feedback group. Examining the subjects' performance of question development in the two posttests, it can be found that 9 of 15 subjects were considered to develop to stage 5 in the group with an enhanced opportunity, and that 5 of 15 subjects were considered to develop to stage 5 in the group with an opportunity to modify, and that only 2 of 16 subjects were considered to have developed to stage 5 in no feedback group. Thus, most subjects have advanced to stage 5 in the group with an enhanced opportunity to modify output

Table 5.4 Subjects of each group question development in the two posttests

Group	Subjects	Treatment condition	QD1[a]	QD2[b]	QD[c]
1	16	No feedback	3	3	2
2	15	Recasts (no opportunity to modify)	6	4	3
3	15	CRs (with opportunity to modify)	7	8	5
4	15	Recasts + CRs (enhanced opportunity to modify)	11	10	9

[a]The number of subjects in each group who have developed into stage 5 on question forms in the immediate posttest
[b]The number of subjects in each group who have developed into stage 5 on question forms in the delayed posttest
[c]The number of subjects in each group who have developed into stage 5 on question forms in the experiment

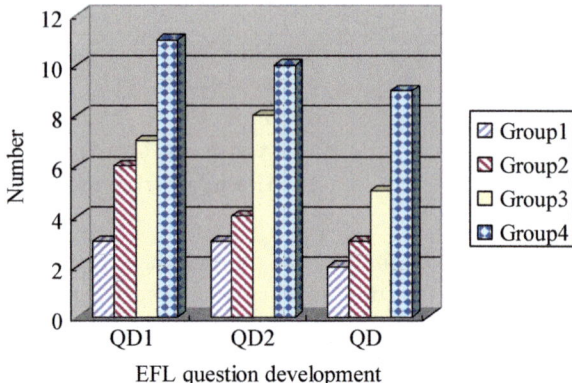

Fig. 5.3 Comparison of EFL question development among groups

among the four groups. Such a tendency can be clearly seen in the two posttests and the final judgment of question formation development, provided in Fig. 5.3.

5.1.3.2 Logistic Regression Analysis Based on QD

Logistic regression is one of the regression statistical methods. According to Hosmer and Lemeshow (1989), "the goal of logistic regression is to find the most appropriate model to describe the relationship between an outcome, a dependent variable, and a set of predictors that act as the independent variables" (cited from McDonough 2005: 90). Logistic regression has many important advantages. Firstly, it can find out the independent variables best predicting the outcomes. Secondly, it can reveal possible interactional effects between independent variables (McDonough 2005; Saito 1999). Lastly, it can keep important individual differences from being obscured by group frequency counts (McDonough 2005). Logistic regression can be adopted when the dependent variable is categorical, different from linear regression requiring a numeric dependent variable (Yu 2007). In the present study, the dependent variable, question development, is binary categorical data; hence, binary logistic regression was employed in data processing.

According to McDonough (2005), Young and Yandell (1999), Yu (2007), there are two general rules in the selection of the independent variables in logistic regression model. One is to predict a set of independent variables which have some relationship with the dependent variable on the basis of related theories. The other is to decide which independent variables are finally selected into logistic regression model on the basis of the univariate statistical analysis of the relationship between each independent variable and the dependent variable. In the present study, based on theories discussed in Chaps. 2 and 3, a set of independent variables were initially selected, including the NF manipulated in the treatment sessions, i.e. recasts and CRs, subjects' attention to question forms during the treatment sessions, the amount of MO with stage 5 questions produced by the subjects in response to the NF in the treatment sessions. Therefore, the logistic regression method has been

5.1 Effects of Negative Feedback, Modified Output, Attention on EFL Development

used to identify whether NF, attention, MO, or all of them are significant predictors of EFL question development, and to demonstrate the most appropriate model composed of the independent variables and the dependent variable.

Univariate Statistical Analysis Based on QD

Prior to manipulating logistic regression, the univariate statistical analysis of the relationship between each independent variable and the dependent variable was conducted. The results are shown in Tables 5.5, 5.6, 5.7, and 5.8.

Because recast, CR, RA, MO, and question development are nominal data, the contingency coefficient in the above four Tables was selected as test result. It can be seen from Table 5.5 that contingency coefficient = 0.185, $p = 0.142 > 0.05$, so the correlation between recast and question development is not significant. As shown in Table 5.6, the contingency coefficient = 0.313, $p = 0.01 < 0.05$, so the correlation between CR and question development is significant at 0.05 level. According to

Table 5.5 Correlation tests between recast and QD

		Value	Asymp. std. error[a]	Approx. T[b]	Approx. sig.
Nominal by nominal	Contingency coefficient	0.185			0.142
Interval by interval	Pearson's R	0.188	0.125	1.471	0.147[c]
Ordinal by ordinal	Spearman correlation	0.188	0.125	1.471	0.147[c]
N of valid cases		61			

[a]Not assuming the null hypothesis
[b]Using the asymptotic standard error assuming the null hypothesis
[c]Based on normal approximation

Table 5.6 Correlation tests between CR and QD

		Value	Asymp. std. error[a]	Approx. T[b]	Approx. sig.
Nominal by nominal	Contingency coefficient	0.313			0.010
Interval by interval	Pearson's R	0.330	0.118	2.682	0.009[c]
Ordinal by ordinal	Spearman correlation	0.330	0.118	2.682	0.009[c]
N of valid cases		61			

[a]Not assuming the null hypothesis
[b]Using the asymptotic standard error assuming the null hypothesis
[c]Based on normal approximation

Table 5.7 Correlation tests between RA and QD

		Value	Asymp. std. error[a]	Approx. T[b]	Approx. sig.
Nominal by nominal	Contingency coefficient	0.370			0.002
Interval by interval	Pearson's R	0.398	0.117	3.336	0.001[c]
Ordinal by ordinal	Spearman correlation	0.398	0.117	3.336	0.001[c]
N of valid cases		61			

[a]Not assuming the null hypothesis
[b]Using the asymptotic standard error assuming the null hypothesis
[c]Based on normal approximation

Table 5.8 Correlation tests between MO and QD

		Value	Asymp. std. error[a]	Approx. T[b]	Approx. sig.
Nominal by nominal	Contingency coefficient	0.540			0.000
Interval by interval	Pearson's R	0.601	0.076	5.771	0.000[c]
Ordinal by ordinal	Spearman correlation	0.597	0.106	5.712	0.000[c]
N of valid cases		61			

[a]Not assuming the null hypothesis
[b]Using the asymptotic standard error assuming the null hypothesis
[c]Based on normal approximation

Table 5.7, contingency coefficient = 0.370, $p = 0.002 < 0.01$, so the correlation between RA and question development is significant at 0.01 level. As seen in Table 5.8, contingency coefficient = 0.540, $p = 0.000 < 0.01$, so the correlation between MO and question development is significant at 0.01 level.

Moreover, the univariate statistical analysis on the relationship between every two independent variables was also conducted. Table 5.9 summarizes the correlation coefficients between every two variables.

In summary, EFL question development is significantly correlated with CR, RA, and MO. In other words, CR, RA, and MO can be included in the QD based logistic regression model.

Logistic Regression Analysis Based on QD

Based on the results of the univariate statistical analysis, the results of logistic regression analysis are revealed in the following section. The independent variables were included in logistic regression model by way of an enter selection method.

5.1 Effects of Negative Feedback, Modified Output, Attention on EFL Development

Table 5.9 Correlation coefficients among variables based on QD

Variable	Recast	CR	RA	MO	QD
Recast	1.00	0.016	0.177	0.259	0.185
CR	0.016	1.00	0.177	0.607**	0.313*
RA	0.177	0.177	1.00	0.219	0.370**
MO	0.259	0.607**	0.219	1.00	0.540**
QD	0.185	0.313*	0.370**	0.540**	1.00

*$p < 0.05$
**$p < 0.01$

Table 5.10 Variables not in the equation based on QD (block 0: beginning block)

			Score	df	Sig.
Step 0	Variables	CR	6.629	1	0.010
		RA	9.683	1	0.002
		MO	22.011	1	0.000
	Overall statistics		24.845	3	0.000

The first step is to verify the significance of the logistic regression model, displayed in Table 5.10.

It can be seen from Table 5.10 that the score of overall statistics $X^2 = 24.845$, $p = 0.000 < 0.01$. This indicates that the logistic regression model is significant. Additionally, the score of CR $X^2 = 6.692$, $p = 0.010 < 0.05$; the score of RA $X^2 = 9.683$, $p = 0.002 < 0.01$; the score of MO $X^2 = 22.011$, $p = 0.000 < 0.01$. These data indicate that the correlation between CR and question development is significant at 0.05 level, and that RA and MO have significant correlation with question development at 0.01 level respectively. The result agrees with the previous univariate statistic analysis.

The second step is to test the significance of the logistic regression model coefficients, shown in Table 5.11.

The results of three tests are the same, $X^2 = 33.665$, $p = 0.000 < 0.001$, which indicates that at least one independent variable in logistic regression model is significant, and that omnibus tests of model coefficients are significant.

Thirdly, we move to test the goodness of fit of the logistic regression model, revealed in Tables 5.12 and 5.13.

As shown in Table 5.12, Nagelkerke $R^2 = 0.597$, that is, the independent variables in logistic regression model can interpret the covariation of the dependent variable in a proportion of 59.7%. In logistic regression model, however,

Table 5.11 Omnibus tests of model coefficients based on QD (Block 1: Method = Enter)

		Chi-square	df	Sig.
Step 1	Step	33.665	3	0.000
	Block	33.665	3	0.000
	Model	33.665	3	0.000

Table 5.12 Model summary based on QD

Step	−2 Log likelihood	Cox and Snell R square	Nagelkerke R square
1	42.009	0.424	0.597

Table 5.13 Hosmer and Lemeshow test based on QD

Step	Chi-square	df	Sig.
1	0.913	4	0.923

Nagelkerke R^2 is just a pseudo R^2. As a result, Hosmer and Lemeshow test should also be conducted to examine the goodness of fit of the model.

Clearly presented in Table 5.13, $p = 0.923 > 0.05$. The result indicates that the difference between the expected value and the observed value of the model is not significant. That is to say, the goodness of fit of the model is appropriate for the following test.

The next step is to show how the logistic regression model predicts question development, presented in Table 5.14.

From the data presented in Table 5.14, we can see that the overall percentage of the logistic regression model predicting the dependent variable, the EFL question development, is 86.9%. Moreover, it is shown that the sensitivity (true positive rate) (Yu 2007: 363) is 68.4%, and the specificity (true negative rate) (Yu 2007: 363) is 95.2%. In other words, the logistic regression model can predict successful question development in a proportion of 68.4%. In contrary, it can predict unsuccessful question development in a proportion of 95.2%. Then, the observed groups and the predicted probabilities are revealed in Fig. 5.4.

As shown in Fig. 5.4, the predicted probability, i.e. the cut value, is 0.50. The symbol "0" represents no question development, while the symbol "1" represents question development. It can be seen clearly that the majority of "0" is distributed over the left of 0.50, and the majority of "1" is distributed over the right of 0.50. This indicates that it is a proper distribution, like a U-shape. The proper distribution also indicates that the dependent variable, EFL question development, can be appropriately predicted by the logistic regression model.

Table 5.14 Prediction of logistic regression model based on QD[a]

Observed			Predicted		
			QD		Percentage correct (%)
			0.00	1.00	
Step 1	QD	0.00	40	2	95.2
		1.00	6	13	68.4
	Overall percentage				86.9

[a]The cut value is 0.500

5.1 Effects of Negative Feedback, Modified Output, Attention on EFL Development

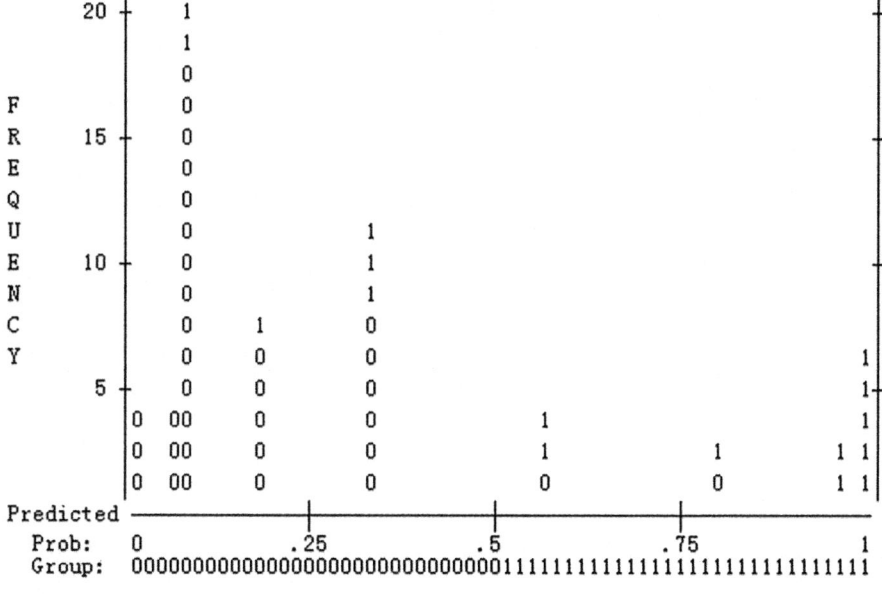

Fig. 5.4 Observed groups and predicted probabilities based on QD

On the basis of the general analysis of the logistic regression model, the final step is to analyze the significance of each independent variable in the logistic regression model, shown in Table 5.15.

The data of Sig. in Table 5.15 indicate the significance of each independent variable in the logistic regression model. Of all the independent variables, RA

Table 5.15 Variables in the equation based on QD

		B	S.E.	Wald	df	Sig.	Exp(B)	95.0% C.I. for Exp(B)	
								Lower	Upper
Step 1[a]	CR	−1.977	1.461	1.830	1	0.176	0.139	0.008	2.429
	RA	1.851	0.832	4.953	1	0.026	6.368	1.247	32.514
	MO	2.946	1.139	6.687	1	0.010	19.039	2.041	177.629
	Constant	−2.577	0.747	11.887	1	0.001	0.076		

[a]Variable(s) entered on step 1: CR, RA, MO

($p = 0.026 < 0.05$) and MO ($p = 0.010 < 0.05$) are significant at 0.05 level, while CR ($p = 0.176 > 0.05$) is not significant. That is to say, RA and MO have significant impact on the EFL question development, but CR has no significant effect on the EFL question development. Furthermore, the data of Exp(B) presented in Table 5.15 demonstrate the contribution of each independent variable to the logistic regression model. Exp(B) refers to odds ratio of the corresponding independent variable. Odds ratio of RA is 6.368, which indicates that the odds of the question development of the subjects with attention to question forms are 6.368 times of that of the subjects without attention to question forms. In the same way, odds ratio of MO is 19.039, which indicates that the odds of the question development of the subjects producing MO are 19.039 times of that of the subjects without producing MO. Therefore, according to the results drawn from the above Table, MO and RA are both significantly predictive of EFL question development. Of the two predictors, MO is a more significant predictor of EFL question development than RA because MO may have more effects on the EFL question development compared with RA.

5.1.3.3 Logistic Regression Analysis Based on QD1

Univariate Statistical Analysis Based on QD1

Before conducting the logistic regression analysis based on EFL question development in the immediate posttest, we should also carry on univariate statistical analysis to find appropriate variables in the QD1 based logistic regression model. Table 5.16 summarizes the correlation coefficients among the variables in the immediate posttest.

The correlation coefficients between independent variable and question development in Table 5.16 indicate that in the immediate posttest, question development is significantly correlated with CR and MO. Therefore, recast and RA should not be included in the logistic regression model. In other words, only CR and MO were kept in the QD1 based logistic regression model.

Table 5.16 Correlation coefficients among variables in immediate posttest

Variable	Recast	CR	RA	MO	QD1
Recast	1.00	0.016	0.177	0.259	0.239
CR	0.016	1.00	0.177	0.607**	0.298*
RA	0.177	0.177	1.00	0.219	0.199
MO	0.259	0.607**	0.219	1.00	0.460**
QD1	0.239	0.298*	0.199	0.460*	1.00

*$p < 0.05$
**$p < 0.01$

5.1 Effects of Negative Feedback, Modified Output, Attention on EFL Development

Logistic Regression Analysis Based on QD1

Firstly, similar to the QD based logistic regression analysis, it is necessary to verify the significance of the QD1 based logistic regression model, shown in Table 5.17.

According to Table 5.17, the score of overall statistics ($X^2 = 13.160$, $p = 0.001 < 0.01$) indicates that the logistic regression model is significant. Moreover, the score of CR ($X^2 = 5.926$, $p = 0.015 < 0.05$) and the score of MO ($X^2 = 12.899$, $p = 0.000 < 0.01$) show that the correlation between CR and QD1, and that between MO and QD1 are significant respectively at 0.05 level and 0.01 level. The result is consistent with the previous univariate statistic analysis.

Secondly, the results of omnibus tests of model coefficients ($X^2 = 33.665$, $p = 0.000 < 0.001$) shown in Table 5.18 indicate that at least one independent variable in logistic regression model is significant, and that the logistic regression model coefficients are significant.

Thirdly, the goodness of fit test ($X^2 = 0.046$, $p = 0.997 > 0.05$) presented in Table 5.19 reveals that the model is appropriate for the following test.

Then, how the logistic regression model predicts QD1 is presented in Table 5.20.

The above Table shows that the overall percentage of the logistic regression model predicting QD1 is 72.1%. The sensitivity (true positive rate) and the specificity (true negative rate) are 59.3 and 82.4%, respectively. In other words, the logistic regression model can predict successful QD1 in a proportion of 59.3%. On the other hand, the model can predict unsuccessful question development in a proportion of 82.4%. In succession, the observed groups and the predicted probabilities are revealed in Fig. 5.4.

It can be seen from Fig. 5.5 that the majority of symbol "0" is distributed over the left of 0.50, and the majority of symbol "1" is distributed over the right of 0.50. Therefore, it is also an appropriate distribution which indicates that QD1 can also be appropriately predicted by the logistic regression model.

Finally, we move to analyze the significance of each independent variable in the logistic regression model, which is shown in Table 5.21.

Of all the independent variables presented in Table 5.21, only MO ($p = 0.027 < 0.05$) is significant at 0.05 level, while CR ($p = 0.746 > 0.05$) is not a significant predictor. In other words, only MO has a significant effect on the EFL question development in the immediate posttest. Moreover, odds ratio of MO (Exp (B) = 3.874) indicates that in the immediate posttest the odds of the question development of subjects producing MO are 3.874 times of that of subjects without producing MO. Hence, according to the data shown in Table 5.21, only MO is significantly predictive of EFL question development in the immediate posttest.

Table 5.17 Variables not in the equation based on QD1 (block 0: beginning block)

			Score	df	Sig.
Step 0	Variables	CR	5.926	1	0.015
		MO	12.899	1	0.000
	Overall statistics		13.160	2	0.001

Table 5.18 Omnibus tests of model coefficients based on QD1 (block 1: Method = Enter)

		Chi-square	df	Sig.
Step 1	Step	17.048	2	0.000
	Block	17.048	2	0.000
	Model	17.048	2	0.000

Table 5.19 Hosmer and Lemeshow test based on QD1

Step	Chi-square	df	Sig.
1	0.046	3	0.997

Table 5.20 Prediction of logistic regression model based on QD1[a]

Observed			Predicted		
			QD1		Percentage correct (%)
			0.00	1.00	
Step 1	QD1	0.00	28	6	82.4
		1.00	11	16	59.3
	Overall percentage				72.1

[a]The cut value is 0.500

5.1.3.4 Logistic Regression Analysis Based on QD2

Univariate Statistical Analysis Based on QD2

Similar with the univariate statistical analysis based on QD1, a univariate statistical analysis was carried out firstly to establish the QD2 based logistic regression model. Table 5.22 shows the correlation coefficients among variables in the delayed posttest.

The correlation coefficients in Table 5.22 indicate that in the delayed posttest question development is significantly correlated with CR, RA and MO. That is to say, recast should not be included in the logistic regression model. On the basis of the delayed posttest results, the logistic regression model comprised CR, RA and MO. This composition is the same as the QD based logistic regression model. After analyzing the QD based and the QD1 based logistic regression models, the QD2 based logistic regression analysis has been presented in the following section.

Logistic Regression Analysis Based on QD2

In the first place, the significance of the QD2 based logistic regression model should also be tested. The test result is shown in Table 5.23.

The score of overall statistics ($X^2 = 21.658$, $p = 0.000 < 0.01$), presented in Table 5.23, indicates that the logistic regression model is significant. Then, the scores of CR ($X^2 = 8.826$, $p = 0.005 < 0.01$), RA ($X^2 = 13.211$, $p = 0.000 < 0.01$) and MO ($X^2 = 13.955$, $p = 0.000 < 0.01$) converge to show that in the delayed

5.1 Effects of Negative Feedback, Modified Output, Attention on EFL Development

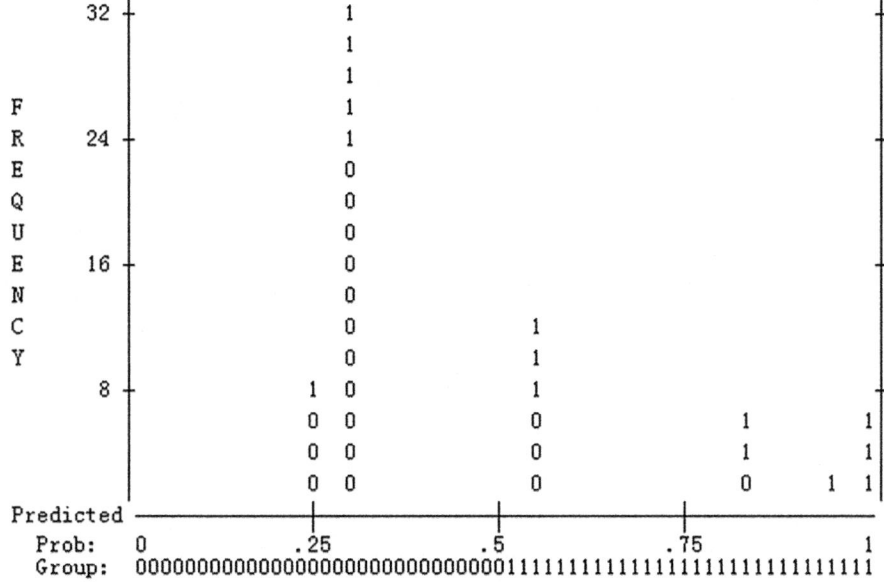

Fig. 5.5 Observed groups and predicted probabilities based on QD1

Table 5.21 Variables in the equation based on QD1

		B	S.E.	Wald	df	Sig.	Exp(B)	95.0% C.I. for Exp(B)	
								Lower	Upper
Step 1[a]	CR	−0.262	0.810	0.105	1	0.746	0.769	0.157	3.765
	MO	1.354	0.612	4.895	1	0.027	3.874	1.167	12.856
	Constant	−0.894	0.396	5.103	1	0.024	0.409		

[a]Variable(s) entered on step 1: CR, MO

posttest EFL question development has significant correlation with CR, RA, and MO, respectively at 0.01 level. The result confirms the previous univariate statistic analysis.

The second step is to conduct the omnibus tests of model coefficients, which is shown in Table 5.24.

Table 5.22 Correlation coefficients among variables in delayed posttest

Variable	Recast	CR	RA	MO	QD2
Recast	1.00	0.016	0.177	0.259	0.113
CR	0.016	1.00	0.177	0.607**	0.356**
RA	0.177	0.177	1.00	0.219	0.422**
MO	0.259	0.607**	0.219	1.00	0.478**
QD2	0.113	0.356**	0.422**	0.478**	1.00

*$p < 0.05$
**$p < 0.01$

Table 5.23 Variables not in the equation based on QD2 (block 0: beginning block)

			Score	df	Sig.
Step 0	Variables	CR	8.826	1	0.003
		RA	13.211	1	0.000
		MO	13.955	1	0.000
	Overall statistics		21.658	3	0.000

Table 5.24 Omnibus tests of model coefficients based on QD2 (block 1: method = enter)

		Chi-square	df	Sig.
Step 1	Step	26.739	3	0.000
	Block	26.739	3	0.000
	Model	26.739	3	0.000

The results of the omnibus tests of model coefficients ($X^2 = 26.739$, $p = 0.000 < 0.001$) shown in Table 5.24 indicate that not only the logistic regression model coefficients are significant, but also at least one independent variable in this logistic regression model is significant.

Then, the Hosmer and Lemeshow test ($X^2 = 2.116$, $p = 0.833 > 0.05$) revealed in Table 5.25 indicates that the goodness of fit of the logistic regression model is quite appropriate for the ensuing tests.

In succession, how the logistic regression model predicts EFL question development in the delayed posttest is presented in Table 5.26.

The overall percentage in Table 5.26 shows that on the whole, the logistic regression model can predict EFL question development in the delayed posttest in a proportion of 80.3%. It can also be seen that the sensitivity (true positive rate) and the specificity (true negative rate) are 64.0 and 91.7%, respectively. Namely, the logistic regression model can predict successful QD2 in a proportion of 64.0%, while it can predict unsuccessful QD2 in a proportion of 91.7%. In the following section, the observed groups and the predicted probabilities are revealed in Fig. 5.6.

As expected, the majority of symbol "0" is distributed over the left of 0.50, and the majority of symbol "1" is distributed over the right of 0.50. Accordingly, it is

Table 5.25 Hosmer and Lemeshow test based on QD2

Step	Chi-square	df	Sig.
1	2.116	5	0.833

5.1 Effects of Negative Feedback, Modified Output, Attention on EFL Development

Table 5.26 Prediction of logistic regression model based on QD2[a]

Observed			Predicted		Percentage correct (%)
			QD2		
			0.00	1.00	
Step 1	QD2	0.00	33	3	91.7
		1.00	9	16	64.0
	Overall percentage				80.3

[a]The cut value is 0.500

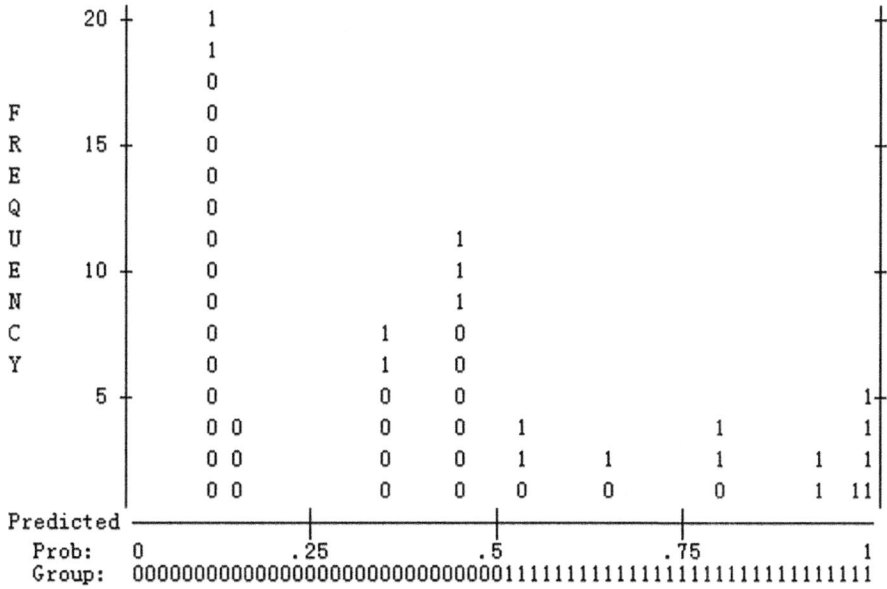

Fig. 5.6 Observed groups and predicted probabilities based on QD2

also an appropriate distribution which indicates that EFL question development can also be appropriately predicted by the QD2 based logistic regression model.

Lastly, we move to analyze the significance of each independent variable in the logistic regression model, the results shown in Table 5.27.

The data of Sig. in Table 5.27 indicate that only RA ($p = 0.005 < 0.01$) is significant at 0.01 level, while neither CR ($p = 0.705 > 0.05$) nor MO ($p = 0.063 > 0.05$) is significant predictor in this logistic regression model. The

Table 5.27 Variables in the equation based on QD2

		B	S.E.	Wald	df	Sig.	Exp(B)	95.0% C.I. for EXP(B)	
								Lower	Upper
Step 1[a]	CR	0.326	0.862	0.143	1	0.705	1.386	0.256	7.513
	RA	1.942	0.691	7.901	1	0.005	6.972	1.800	27.000
	MO	1.203	0.646	3.468	1	0.063	3.332	0.939	11.822
	Constant	−2.154	0.621	12.008	1	0.001	0.116		

[a]Variable(s) entered on step 1: CR, RA, MO

results reveal that only RA has a significant effect on the EFL question development in the delayed posttest. Furthermore, odds ratio of RA (Exp(B) = 6.972) suggests that in the delayed posttest the odds of the question development of subjects reporting attention to question forms are 6.972 times of that of subjects without reporting attention to question forms. Therefore, according to the data shown in Table 5.27, only RA is significantly predictive of the EFL question development in the delayed posttest.

5.1.4 Summary

To summarize, firstly the logistic regression is employed to indicate whether NF, RA, MO are significantly predictive of EFL question development, and to demonstrate what effects these predictors have on EFL question development. Prior to the logistic regression analysis based on QD, the appropriate independent variables, i.e. CR, RA, and MO, for the logistic regression model were selected through univariate statistic analysis. After the model established, the model coefficients were tested to be significant. Additionally, the goodness of fit test of the model indicated that the model was appropriate for the successive logistic regression analysis. After that, the model was proved to be able to predict the EFL question development in a proportion of 86.9%. And finally, the most important Table 5.15 shows that RA and MO have significant effects on EFL question development, and that MO has a more significant effect on EFL question development than RA.

Secondly, with the same process of the logistic regression analysis based on QD, we have gained a somewhat different result concerning the EFL question development in the immediate posttest. Generally, the differences lie in two aspects. One aspect is on the components included in the two logistic regression models. The logistic regression model based on QD is composed of three predictors, i.e. CR, RA, and MO, while the logistic regression model based on QD1 is composed of only two predictors, i.e. CR and MO. The other aspect is on the predictive ability of the dependent variable. In the logistic regression model based on QD, MO and RA are both significant predictors of QD, whereas in the logistic regression model based on QD1, MO is the only significant predictor of QD1.

5.1 Effects of Negative Feedback, Modified Output, Attention on EFL Development   89

Lastly, both dissimilarities and similarities have been found by comparing the results of the logistic regression analysis based on QD2 with the previous logistic regression analyses based on QD and QD1. On the one hand, the components of the logistic regression models based on QD and QD2 are the same, involving three independent variables, i.e. CR, RA, and MO, while the logistic regression model based on QD1 only comprises two independent variables, i.e. CR and MO. On the other hand, although the logistic regression models based on QD and QD2 involve the same expected predictors, the significant predictors in the two models are different. In QD based logistic regression model, RA and MO are the significant predictors of the EFL question development, whereas in QD2 based logistic regression model only RA is significantly predictive of the EFL question development in the delayed posttest. As for QD1 based logistic regression model, only MO is the significant predictor of the EFL question development in the immediate posttest. Here is an interesting phenomenon: in the immediate posttest, only MO has a significant effect on QD1, and in the delayed posttest, only RA has a significant effect on QD2, while both MO and RA have significant effects on QD.

5.2 Effects of Learners' Perceptions on EFL Development

As previously stated in Chap. 4, the data of the EFL learners' perception about NF and question development were analyzed to investigate research question 4, that is, the EFL learners' perception about NF employed in the study and its effect on EFL question development.

5.2.1 Data Input in SPSS

The data of the EFL learners' perceptions about NF and question development were input subject by subject in SPSS data set, in which there were also 10 variables, including group, number, perception category (PC) 1, PC2, PC3, PC4, PC5, QD1, QD2, and QD. Figure 5.7 is an example of the perception data input in SPSS of the second group of subjects.

5.2.2 The EFL Learners' Perception About NF

All the subjects in the experiment except for the subjects in the first group participated in the stimulated recall session because the first group was treated under the condition of no feedback. It has been mentioned in Chap. 4 that the second group of subjects was treated under the condition of providing recasts as NF, the third group of subjects was treated under the condition of providing CRs as NF, and

	group	number	pc1	pc2	pc3	pc4	pc5	qd1	qd2	qd
1	2.00	17.00	5.00	2.00	.00	6.00	.00	.00	.00	.00
2	2.00	18.00	6.00	5.00	3.00	1.00	.00	.00	1.00	.00
3	2.00	19.00	4.00	1.00	1.00	2.00	.00	1.00	1.00	1.00
4	2.00	20.00	3.00	2.00	.00	1.00	.00	1.00	.00	.00
5	2.00	21.00	5.00	2.00	.00	4.00	1.00	.00	.00	.00
6	2.00	22.00	10.00	7.00	2.00	1.00	.00	.00	.00	.00
7	2.00	23.00	4.00	5.00	2.00	.00	.00	1.00	.00	.00
8	2.00	24.00	2.00	1.00	.00	1.00	1.00	1.00	1.00	1.00
9	2.00	25.00	4.00	3.00	.00	17.00	.00	.00	.00	.00
10	2.00	26.00	4.00	.00	4.00	5.00	2.00	1.00	.00	.00
11	2.00	27.00	1.00	1.00	.00	14.00	2.00	.00	.00	.00
12	2.00	28.00	2.00	1.00	1.00	.00	1.00	.00	.00	.00
13	2.00	29.00	5.00	1.00	3.00	.00	1.00	1.00	1.00	1.00
14	2.00	30.00	3.00	7.00	7.00	.00	2.00	.00	.00	.00
15	2.00	31.00	14.00	1.00	.00	.00	1.00	.00	.00	.00
16	2.00	32.00	.00	1.00	.00	5.00	5.00	1.00	1.00	1.00

Fig. 5.7 Perception data input in SPSS of the second group

the fourth group of subjects was treated under the condition of providing recasts with open-ended CRs as NF. Therefore, we intend to analyze how the EFL learners under the above three treatment conditions perceive NF.

5.2.2.1 The EFL Learners' Perception Analysis Within Group

The EFL learners' perception about NF in each group has been analyzed firstly.

The Second Group of EFL Learners' Perception About Recasts

During treatment period, the 15 EFL learners in the second group received 197 recasts as NF, which can be seen from Fig. 5.2. Accordingly through stimulated recall, the 15 EFL learners described how they perceived these recasts at that time. Under this treatment condition their perceptions were classified into five categories, that is, (1) the instructor was correcting my grammatical errors, such as "通过老师说的，我感觉出自己有错误"; (2) the instructor did not understand what I said, such as "可能老师没太明白我说的"; (3) the instructor is helping me to finish the task, such as "我觉得老师好像想帮我把问题说得更完整"; (4) I did not notice what the instructor said, but was thinking how to continue the task, such as "我当时在想通过问题确定其所属年龄层，所以没有注意老师说的话"; (5) I did not remember the situation at that time, such as "这段不记得了".

Table 5.28 reveals the frequency and percentage of each category of the EFL learners' perception about NF in the second group.

Apparently shown in Table 5.28, the most recasts (36.5%) were perceived as correcting the EFL learners' grammatical errors. Fewer recasts (26.4%) were neglected because the EFL learners fixed their attention on the tasks. Much fewer recasts (19.8%) were misunderstood as a request for the EFL learners to clarify their

5.2 Effects of Learners' Perceptions on EFL Development

Table 5.28 The EFL learners' perception about recasts group 2

PC	1	2	3	4	5	Total
Frequency of recasts	72	39	23	52	11	197
Percentage	36.5%	19.8%	11.7%	26.4%	5.6%	100%

utterances. The minority of recasts (11.7%) was perceived as helping them to finish the task. 5.6% of recasts in the interactional episodes were forgotten by the EFL learners. These data indicate that the frequency and percentage order of the EFL learners' perception of recasts in this group is PC1 > PC4 > PC2 > PC3 > PC5.

Although Table 5.28 shows the difference of frequency and percentage among perception categories, it is necessary to do further investigation about whether the differences are significant. The results of paired sample test of PC in the second group are summarized in Table 5.29.

As shown in Table 5.29, the differences between PC 1 and 2 ($p = 0.035 < 0.05$), 1 and 3 ($p = 0.007 < 0.05$), 1 and 5 ($p = 0.001 < 0.05$), and 2 and 5 ($p = 0.015 < 0.05$), respectively are significant. Obviously, PC1 is most significantly different from other categories. It may be tentatively demonstrated that recasts, in general terms, would be considered as grammatical error correction by the EFL learners.

The Third Group of EFL Learners' Perception About CRs

The 15 EFL learners in the third group received 154 CRs as NF in treatment tasks, which can also be seen in Fig. 5.2. By way of the stimulated recall, the 15 EFL learners recollected how they perceived these CRs during the treatment period.

Table 5.29 Paired samples test of PC in group 2

		Paired differences					t	df	Sig. (2-tailed)
		Mean	Std. deviation	Std. error mean	95% confidence interval of the difference				
					Lower	Upper			
Pair 1	PC 1–2	2.2000	3.64887	0.94214	0.1793	4.2207	2.335	14	0.035
Pair 2	PC 1–3	3.2667	3.99046	1.03033	1.0568	5.4765	3.170	14	0.007
Pair 3	PC 1–4	1.3333	6.96590	1.79859	−2.5243	5.1909	0.741	14	0.471
Pair 4	PC 1–5	4.0667	3.57505	0.92307	2.0869	6.0465	4.406	14	0.001
Pair 5	PC 2–3	1.0667	2.15362	0.55606	−0.1260	2.2593	1.918	14	0.076
Pair 6	PC 2–4	−0.8667	6.15127	1.58825	−4.2731	2.5398	−0.546	14	0.594
Pair 7	PC 2–5	1.8667	2.61498	0.67518	0.4185	3.3148	2.765	14	0.015
Pair 8	PC 3–4	−1.9333	6.28452	1.62266	−5.4136	1.5469	−1.191	14	0.253
Pair 9	PC 3–5	0.8000	1.85934	0.48008	−0.2297	1.8297	1.666	14	0.118
Pair 10	PC 4–5	2.7333	5.27076	1.36091	−0.1855	5.6522	2.008	14	0.064

Under this treatment condition their perceptions were classified into four categories, without PC3, i.e. 'the instructor is helping me to finish the task'. The four categories are: (1) the instructor was correcting my grammatical errors, such as "听完老师问我, 我意识到自己出错了"; (2) the instructor did not understand what I said, such as "可能由于我的发音, 老师没听清楚我说的, 就让我再说一遍"; (4) I did not notice what the instructor said, but was thinking how to continue the task, such as "我当时在想怎么把问题问的再清楚一点儿, 就没有注意老师说的话"; (5) I did not remember the situation at that time, such as "不记得了".

Table 5.30 shows the frequency and percentage of the each category of the EFL learners' perception about CRs in the third group.

It can be seen from Table 5.30 that the category of perception in group 3 is different from that in group 2. Obviously, in the third group no CRs were perceived as a help for the EFL learners to complete the task. Moreover, most CRs (51.3%) were not considered as correcting the EFL learners' grammatical errors, but as a request to clarify their utterances. The second-most CRs (24.7%) were perceived as correcting grammatical errors. Much fewer CRs (16.9%) were ignored for the EFL learners focused on the task. In the same way, the EFL learners failed to remember the interactional episodes involving the least CRs (7.1%). Therefore, the data indicate that the frequency and percentage order of the EFL learners' perception about CRs is PC2 > PC1 > PC4 > PC5.

Furthermore, we move to examine the significance of the differences among perception categories. Table 5.31 presents the results of paired sample test of PC in the third group.

Revealed in Table 5.31, the differences between PC 2 and 1 ($p = 0.003 < 0.05$), 2 and 4 ($p = 0.005 < 0.05$), 2 and 5 ($p = 0.001 < 0.05$), and 1 and 5 ($p = 0.036 < 0.05$) are significant, respectively. These data indicate that PC 2 is the most significantly different from other categories. Accordingly, it is suggested that CRs would be perceived as a request to clarify the EFL learners' utterances in most situations.

The Fourth Group of EFL Learners' Perception About Recasts + CRs

Through treatment period, the 15 EFL learners in the fourth group received 156 recasts + CRs as NF, seen in Fig. 5.2. According to the 15 EFL learners' description about how they perceived recasts + CRs during the treatment sessions, their perceptions under this treatment condition were classified into five categories. They are: (1) the instructor was correcting my grammatical errors, such as "当时听

Table 5.30 The EFL learners' perception about CRs in group 3	PC	1	2	4	5	Total
	Frequency of recasts	38	79	26	11	154
	Percentage	24.7%	51.3%	16.9%	7.1%	100%

5.2 Effects of Learners' Perceptions on EFL Development

Table 5.31 Paired samples test of PC in the group 3

		Paired differences					t	df	Sig. (2-tailed)
		Mean	Std. deviation	Std. error mean	95% confidence interval of the difference				
					Lower	Upper			
Pair 1	PC 1–2	−2.6667	2.87021	0.74108	−4.2561	−1.0772	−3.598	14	0.003
Pair 2	PC 1–4	0.8000	3.62925	0.93707	−1.2098	2.8098	0.854	14	0.408
Pair 3	PC 1–5	1.8000	3.00476	0.77583	0.1360	3.4640	2.320	14	0.036
Pair 4	PC 2–4	3.4667	3.97971	1.02756	1.2628	5.6706	3.374	14	0.005
Pair 5	PC 2–5	4.4667	3.85202	0.99459	2.3335	6.5998	4.491	14	0.001
Pair 6	PC 4–5	1.0000	2.07020	0.53452	−0.1464	2.1464	1.871	14	0.082

了老师的话就觉得可能是自己说的有问题,老师在帮我纠正"; (2) the instructor did not understand what I said, such as "当时就觉得老师没听明白我说的,所以让我再重复一遍"; (3) the instructor is helping me to finish the task, such as "当时我不会表达想问的,老师的话好像是在帮我往下说"; (4) I did not notice what the instructor said, but was thinking how to continue the task, such as "我当时在想这个问题可能让老师不太好回答,就没有注意听老师说的话"; (5) I did not remember the situation at that time, such as "不记得了".

It is presented in Table 5.32 that the frequency and percentage of each category of the EFL learners' perceptions about the NF in the fourth group.

Clearly, the category of perception in the fourth group is the same with that in the second group. According to Table 5.32, the most recasts + CRs (55.1%) were regarded as correcting grammatical errors. Fewer recasts + CRs (24.4%) were not attended to because the EFL learners concentrated on their tasks. Much fewer recasts + CRs (24.4%) were misconceived as a request for the utterance clarification. Only 5.1% of recasts + CRs involved in the interactional episodes were forgotten by the EFL learners. A smallest part of recasts + CRs (1.9%) were perceived as helping them with the task. These data indicate that the frequency and percentage order of the EFL learners' perception about recasts + CRs is PC1 > PC4 > PC2 > PC5 > PC3. However, the order is found somewhat different from that in the second group, in the percentages of PC5 and PC3.

Moreover, it is indispensable to verify the significance of the differences among perception categories. A paired sample test was also conducted to show the result, seen in Table 5.33.

As identified in Table 5.33, the significant differences lie in PC 1 and 2 ($p = 0.001 < 0.05$), 1 and 3 ($p = 0.000 < 0.05$), 1 and 4 ($p = 0.004 < 0.05$), 1 and 5 ($p = 0.000 < 0.05$), 2 and 3 ($p = 0.004 < 0.05$), 3 and 4 ($p = 0.002 < 0.05$), and

Table 5.32 The EFL learners' perception about recasts + CRs in group 4

PC	1	2	3	4	5	Total
Frequency of recasts	86	21	3	38	8	156
Percentage	55.1%	13.5%	1.9%	24.4%	5.1%	100%

Table 5.33 Paired samples test of PC in group 4

		Paired differences					t	df	Sig. (2-tailed)
		Mean	Std. deviation	Std. error mean	95% confidence interval of the difference				
					Lower	Upper			
Pair 1	PC 1–2	4.3333	4.11733	1.06309	2.0532	6.6134	4.076	14	0.001
Pair 2	PC 1–3	5.5333	3.39888	0.87759	3.6511	7.4156	6.305	14	0.000
Pair 3	PC 1–4	3.2000	3.60951	0.93197	1.2011	5.1989	3.434	14	0.004
Pair 4	PC 1–5	5.2000	3.56971	0.92170	3.2232	7.1768	5.642	14	0.000
Pair 5	PC 2–3	1.2000	1.37321	0.35456	0.4395	1.9605	3.384	14	0.004
Pair 6	PC 2–4	−1.1333	2.61498	0.67518	−2.5815	0.3148	−1.679	14	0.115
Pair 7	PC 2–5	0.8667	2.41622	0.62386	−0.4714	2.2047	1.389	14	0.186
Pair 8	PC 3–4	−2.3333	2.35028	0.60684	−3.6349	−1.0318	−3.845	14	0.002
Pair 9	PC 3–5	−0.3333	1.54303	0.39841	−1.1878	0.5212	−0.837	14	0.417
Pair 10	PC 4–5	2.0000	2.32993	0.60159	0.7097	3.2903	3.325	14	0.005

4 and 5 ($p = 0.005 < 0.05$), respectively. Clearly, PC 1 is most significantly different from other categories. Thus, it can be tentatively drawn that recasts + CRs would be generally perceived as grammatical error correction by the EFL learners.

To sum up, according to the stimulated recall data, the EFL learners' perceptions of the NF can be classified into five categories, consisting of an error correction, a request for clarification, a guide in task completion, being ignored, and being forgotten. All the five categories can be seen in all the groups except for group 3. It should be noted that in group 3, no CRs were perceived as a guide in task completion. Paired samples tests of PC in each group indicate that the differences among perception categories in each group are significant. Therefore, it can be tentatively concluded that in most cases recasts and recasts + CRs are considered as error correction, while CRs are deemed as a request for utterance clarification.

5.2.2.2 The EFL Learners' Perception Analysis Between Groups

After analyzing the EFL learners' perceptions about NF in each group, we intend to do further exploration on the perceptions about NF between groups. ANOVA analysis was conducted to identify the differences of each PC between groups. The results are presented below in Table 5.34.

Table 5.34 shows that the differences of PC1 ($p = 0.034 < 0.05$), PC2 ($p = 0.034 < 0.05$), and PC3 ($p = 0.034 < 0.05$) are significant between groups. In other words, PC1, PC2, and PC3 are significant categories of the EFL learners' perceptions about the NF.

Subsequently, Post Hoc tests were conducted to gain deeper insight into the differences of PC1, PC2, and PC3 between every two groups. Before that, homogeneity of variances should be tested firstly.

5.2 Effects of Learners' Perceptions on EFL Development

Table 5.34 ANOVA analysis between groups

		Sum of squares	df	Mean square	F	Sig.
PC1	Between groups	66.521	2	33.260	3.659	0.034
PC2	Between groups	129.700	2	64.850	12.319	0.000
PC3	Between groups	18.640	2	9.320	5.728	0.006
PC4	Between groups	31.807	2	15.903	1.327	0.276
PC5	Between groups	2.838	2	1.419	1.080	0.349

It can be found in Table 5.35 that the variances of PC1 ($p = 0.461 > 0.05$) and PC2 ($p = 0.210 > 0.05$) are equal while the variance of PC3 ($p = 0.000 < 0.05$) is unequal. Therefore, in Post Hoc test LSD method was selected for PC1 and PC2, whereas Tamhane method was selected for PC3. The results of multiple comparisons are presented below.

According to Table 5.36, as for PC1 significant difference exists neither between groups 2 and 3 ($p = 0.113 > 0.05$) nor between groups 2 and 4 ($p = 0.216 > 0.05$), but it does exist between groups 3 and 4 ($p = 0.010 < 0.05$). As aforementioned, the NF provided for group 3 and group 4 is respectively CRs and recasts + CRs. The above data on PC1 indicate that recasts and CRs alone are not significantly different in the learners' perceiving NF as error correction. On the other hand, CRs and recasts + CRs are significantly different in the learners' perceiving NF as error correction. Thus, it may be inferred that recasts + CRs would be more likely to be perceived as error correction.

Then, as for PC2 significant difference appears both between groups 2 and 3 ($p = 0.001 < 0.05$) and between groups 3 and 4 ($p = 0.000 < 0.05$), while it does not appear between groups 2 and 4 ($p = 0.189 > 0.05$). As previously stated, the NF provided for group 2 is recasts. The significant difference of PC2 between groups 2 and 3 indicates that CRs and recasts are significantly different in the learners' perceiving NF as a request for utterance clarification. The same result can also be found between CRs and recasts + CRs. Therefore, it can be suggested that CR alone would be more likely to be regarded as a request for clarification, compared with recasts and recasts + CRs, respectively. Additionally, since the difference of PC2 between groups 2 and 4 is not significant, recasts and recasts + CRs do not lead to differences in the EFL learners' perceiving NF as a request for clarification.

Finally as for PC3, significant difference can only be found between groups 2 and 3 ($p = 0.034 < 0.05$), whereas no significant differences are found either between groups 2 and 4 ($p = 0.095 > 0.05$) or between groups 3 and 4 ($p = 0.705 > 0.05$).

Table 5.35 Test of homogeneity of variances

	Levene statistic	df1	df2	Sig.
PC1	0.789	2	42	0.461
PC2	1.620	2	42	0.210
PC3	14.950	2	42	0.000

Table 5.36 Multiple comparisons by post Hoc tests

Dependent variable		(I) group	(J) group	Mean difference (I–J)	Std. error	Sig.	95% confidence interval	
							Lower bound	Upper bound
PC1	LSD	2.00	3.00	1.7857	1.10338	0.113	−0.4410	4.0124
			4.00	−1.2333	1.08359	0.261	−3.4201	0.9534
		3.00	2.00	−1.7857	1.10338	0.113	−4.0124	0.4410
			4.00	−3.0190*	1.12041	0.010	−5.2801	−0.7580
		4.00	2.00	1.2333	1.08359	0.261	−0.9534	3.4201
			3.00	3.0190*	1.12041	0.010	0.7580	5.2801
PC2	LSD	2.00	3.00	−3.0000*	0.83967	0.001	−4.6945	−1.3055
			4.00	1.1000	0.82460	0.189	−0.5641	2.7641
		3.00	2.00	3.0000*	0.83967	0.001	1.3055	4.6945
			4.00	4.1000*	0.85263	0.000	2.3793	5.8207
		4.00	2.00	−1.1000	0.82460	0.189	−2.7641	0.5641
			3.00	−4.1000*	0.85263	0.000	−5.8207	−2.3793
PC3	Tamhane	2.00	3.00	1.4375*	0.49974	0.034	0.0956	2.7794
			4.00	1.2375	0.53827	0.095	−0.1668	2.6418
		3.00	2.00	−1.4375*	0.49974	0.034	−2.7794	−0.0956
			4.00	−0.2000	0.20000	0.705	−0.7418	0.3418
		4.00	2.00	−1.2375	0.53827	0.095	−2.6418	0.1668
			3.00	0.2000	0.20000	0.705	−0.3418	0.7418

*The mean difference is significant at the 0.05 level

Since in group 3 no CRs were considered as PC3, it may cause the significant difference between groups 2 and 3. Therefore, the conclusion can not be safely drawn that providing recasts is significantly correlated with learners' perceiving them as a guide for task completion. As presented in Table 5.32, PC3 only occupies a percentage of 1.9% in group 4, which may be the reason that there is no significant difference between groups 3 and 4. Moreover, no significant difference between groups 2 and 4 may indicate that recasts and recasts + CRs do not significantly affect the EFL learners' perceiving NF as a guide for task completion.

5.2.3 The EFL Learners' Perception About NF and Question Development

In this section, we move to explore the relationship between the learners' perception and their EFL question development. Since PC1, PC2, and PC3 are found significant categories, PC4 and PC5 are not analyzed here.

5.2 Effects of Learners' Perceptions on EFL Development

Table 5.37 Chi-square tests of PC1 and QD

	Value	df	Asymp. sig. (2-sided)	Monte Carlo sig. (2-sided)		
				Sig.	99% confidence interval	
					Lower bound	Upper bound
Pearson chi-square	9.878[a]	12	0.627	0.739[b]	0.728	0.751
Likelihood ratio	12.475	12	0.408	0.726[b]	0.715	0.738
Fisher's exact test	9.548			0.749[b]	0.738	0.760
Linear-by-Linear Association	0.145[c]	1	0.703	0.744[b]	0.733	0.756
N of valid cases	45					

[a]25 cells (96.2%) have expected count less than 5. The minimum expected count is 0.38
[b]Based on 10,000 sampled tables with starting seed 1,502,173,562
[c]The standardized statistic is 0.381

Chi-square tests have been conducted in order to find whether EFL question development has significant correlation with PC1, PC2, and PC3, respectively. The results are displayed below.

Tables 5.37, 5.38, and 5.39 show that due to the minimum expected count less than 5 in all the three chi-square tests, Monte Carlo method was selected. The data of Monte Carlo sig. in the above three Tables indicate that PC1 ($X^2 = 9.878$, $p = 0.739 > 0.05$), PC2 ($X^2 = 10.506$, $p = 0.323 > 0.05$), and PC3 ($X^2 = 3.640$, $p = 0.789 > 0.05$) have no significant relationship with the EFL question development. The results suggest that in this experiment the EFL question development can not be significantly affected by how the EFL learners perceive the provided NF, i.e. recasts, CRs, and recasts + CRs.

Table 5.38 Chi-square tests of PC2 and QD

	Value	df	Asymp. sig. (2-sided)	Monte Carlo sig. (2-sided)		
				Sig.	99% confidence interval	
					Lower bound	Upper bound
Pearson Chi-square	10.506[a]	9	0.311	0.323[b]	0.311	0.335
Likelihood ratio	12.906	9	0.167	0.321[b]	0.309	0.333
Fisher's exact test	9.337			0.390[b]	0.377	0.402
Linear-by-Linear Association	2.369[c]	1	0.124	0.128[b]	0.119	0.136
N of valid cases	45					

[a]19 cells (95.0%) have expected count less than 5. The minimum expected count is 0.38
[b]Based on 10,000 sampled tables with starting seed 1,335,104,164
[c]The standardized statistic is −1.539

Table 5.39 Chi-square tests of PC3 and QD

	Value	df	Asymp. sig. (2-sided)	Monte Carlo sig. (2-sided)		
				Sig.	99% confidence interval	
					Lower bound	Upper bound
Pearson Chi-Square	3.640[a]	5	0.602	0.799[b]	0.789	0.810
Likelihood Ratio	4.961	5	0.421	0.781[b]	0.771	0.792
Fisher's Exact Test	3.549			0.819[b]	0.809	0.828
Linear-by-Linear Association	0.381[c]	1	0.537	0.625[b]	0.612	0.637
N of Valid Cases	45					

[a]10 cells (83.3%) have expected count less than 5. The minimum expected count is 0.38
[b]Based on 10,000 sampled tables with starting seed 79,654,295
[c]The standardized statistic is −0.617

5.2.4 Summary

To summarize, the EFL learners' perceptions about NF in this experiment can generally be classified into five categories: (1) an error correction, (2) a request for clarification, (3) a guide for task completion, (4) being neglected, (5) being forgotten. The EFL learners' perception in groups 2 and 4 involves all the five categories, while in group 3 it does not involve PC 3.

The first step is to analyze the EFL learners' perception about various types of NF provided in the experiment. On the one hand, the five categories of perception were analyzed within groups 2, 3, and 4. Variant PC orders can be found in each group. The majority of NF, recasts in group 2 and recasts + CRs in group 4, was perceived as error correction, while in group 3 the majority of NF, CRs, was regarded as a request for utterance clarification. On the other hand, the five categories of the EFL learners' perception were analyzed between groups. The results of ANOVA analysis indicate that PC1, PC2, and PC3 are significant categories. Furthermore, Post Hoc tests of PC1, PC2, and PC3 suggest that recasts + CRs would be more likely to be considered as an error correction than CRs alone, and that CRs alone would be more likely to be regarded as a request for utterance clarification than recasts or recasts + CRs. Additionally, no CRs were perceived as a guide for task completion in group 3, so that it is far from being able to draw the conclusion that providing recasts is significantly correlated with the learners' perceiving them as a guide for task completion.

The second step is to identify the relationship between the significant perception categories, i.e. PC1, PC2, and PC3, and the question development. The results of Chi-square tests reveal that no significant relationship appears between the EFL question development and PC1, PC2, PC3, respectively. In other words, the learners' perception of NF in this experiment is not a significant predictor of EFL question development. However, it is far from being able to draw a general conclusion that there is no relationship between learners' perception about the NF and EFL question development.

5.3 Interaction Process and Foreign Language Development

All the above findings have been discussed amply in this section.

5.3.1 MO and EFL Development

In the study, statistical analysis has indicated that MO is a significant predictor of EFL development. This result corroborates the Output Hypothesis (Swain 1985, 1993, 1995, 1998) in a certain degree. Swain (1985: 249) proposed that output "may be the trigger that forces the learner to pay attention to the means of expression needed in order to successfully convey his or her own intended meaning". As aforementioned, Izumi (2003) posited that the psycholinguistic basis of Output Hypothesis was Levelt's speech production model (Levelt 1989; Levelt et al. 1999), the most influential one. The significant effects of MO on EFL development can be construed through reference to this model.

Levelt's speech production model, originally identifying a process in which a concept is encoded in a speech form to be communicated, involves conceptualizing, formulating, articulating, and monitoring. Levelt's production model is not intended to account for language learning per se, whereas it can throw some light on how language learning may be brought about through production processes (de Bot 1996; Kormos 1999). Izumi (2003: 168) argued that "the processes of grammatical encoding during production and monitoring to check the matching of the communicative intention and the output enable language learners to assess the possibilities and limitations of their interlanguage capability". In production processes the grammatical encoding requires the speaker's focus on syntactic form. In that case, the speaker has few opportunities to escape grammatical components in the course of production (Izumi 2003). Therefore to modify output encourages the learners to move from "the semantic processing prevalent in comprehension to the syntactic processing needed for production" (Swain and Lapkin 1995: 375). To put it another way, the grammatical encoding in output modification processes may function as "an internal priming device for consciousness raising for the learners, which in turn creates an optimal condition for language learning to take place" (Izumi 2003: 168).

Furthermore, the result of the notable effects of MO on EFL development found in the present study is consistent with McDonough's (2005) study. As expected, in the present study the learners in the two groups without modification opportunities did not modify their previous output, whereas the learners in the two groups with modification opportunities did modify their previous utterances. Additionally, the learners in the group with an enhanced opportunity produced MO with more stage 5 questions than the learners did in the group with a modification opportunity. This indicates that enhancing the modification opportunity promotes the learners' production of more target-like language forms. The analysis of the data from the learners in the group with an enhanced opportunity as follows elucidates the relationships among the NF, MO, and EFL development.

The majority of learners (N = 9) in the enhanced opportunity group has advanced to stage 5 in the question developmental sequence. Pieces of the interactional episodes between Learner 51, for example, and the instructor are shown in (1) below. Learner 51, classified at stage 4 at the beginning of the study, has advanced to stage 5 in the two posttests.

(1) a. Learner 51: Why they meet?   ← Stage 3 question
    Instructor: Why did they meet? Pardon?
    Learner 51: Why did they meet?   ← Stage 5 question
  b. Learner 51: Why they can talk at the first meet?   ← Stage 3 question
    Instructor: Why could they talk at the first meet? Sorry?
    Learner 51: Why can they talk at their first meeting?   ← Stage 5 question
  c. Learner 51: What they study in university?   ← Stage 3 question
    Instructor: What do they study? Pardon?
    Learner 51: What do they study in the university?   ← Stage 5 question
  d. Learner 51: Why the woman ask the man to go to the village?   ← Stage 3 question
    Instructor: Why did the girl ask the boy? Pardon?
    Learner 51: Why did the woman ask the man to go to the village with her?   ← Stage 5 question

In the above four interactional episodes, recasts followed by open-ended CRs were employed by the instructor to enhance the opportunity of Learner 51 to modify her output. As expected, Learner 51 succeeded in modifying her output after the instructor's NF. Insomuch as Learner 51 just repeated the instructor's recasts in (1)(a) and (1)(c), we may doubt that the correct form in the recasts might not be internalized by the learner. Nevertheless, in (1)(b) and (1)(d) Learner 51 did not perform a word-for-word repetition of the instructor's recast, but adopted the question form in the instructor's recasts, i.e. to add or move an auxiliary verb ahead of the subject. The modification behavior indicates that Learner 51 has been aware of her grammatical error so that she reformulated her output and produced stage 5 questions. Although Learner 51 had been virtually taught question formation rules before she was enrolled in the university, she still needed to develop to a higher stage in the question developmental sequence. Then, without recasts followed by CRs as a priming device she could not produce the question forms of a higher stage. Therefore, during the interactional process the instructor may enhance the learner's opportunity to modify her output through recasts followed by CRs, so as to help the

5.3 Interaction Process and Foreign Language Development

learner to strengthen and internalize the interlanguage knowledge about question forms of a higher stage. As de Bot (1996) proposed, output can facilitate the process of the transition of declarative knowledge to procedural knowledge though it does not create completely new declarative knowledge.

However, the minority of learners (N = 6) in the enhanced opportunity group has not advanced to stage 5 in the question developmental sequence. Pieces of the interactional episodes between Learner 54, for instance, and the instructor are shown in (2) below. Learner 54, beginning the study also at stage 4 in the question developmental sequence, has not yet advanced to stage 5 in the two posttests.

(2) a. Learner 54 : Does the door open? ← Stage 4 question
   Instructor: Is the door open? Pardon?
   Learner 54 : The door on the left open or close? ← Stage 2 question
 b. Learner 54 : The girl worries what? ← Stage 2 question
   Instructor: What did this girl worry about? Pardon?
   Learner 54 : Beg your pardon? ← Stage 2 question
 c. Learner 54 : What's the man ...the man is saying what to the old woman? ← Stage 3 question
   Instructor: What is the man saying to the old woman? Pardon?
   Learner 54 : Does he work for the woman? ← Stage 3 question
 d. Learner 54 : Why do they in the village? ← Stage 3 question
   Instructor: Why are they in the village? Pardon?
   Learner 54 : They come to the village to do what? ← Stage 2 question

In the above four interactional episodes, the opportunity of Learner 54 to modify her output was also enhanced through recasts followed by open-ended CRs, whereas she failed to produce target-like question forms involved in recasts in the ensuing output. The learning journal of Learner 54 indicated that she did not notice the question forms in the instructor's NF. Consequently, she has not modified her previous utterance in response to the instructor's NF in an expected way. The interactional episodes of (2)a and (2)d reveal that Learner 54, unaware of the difference between her deviant utterance and target-like question forms in recasts, mistook the instructor's NF for a request for clarification. Thus, she tried to clarify her utterance in the successive output by changing to another expression with the same meaning. The interactional episode of (2)b indicates that Learner 54 did not comprehend the instructor's intention so that she could not produce target-like question form in the successive output. As for the interactional episode of (2)c, Learner 54 failed to understand the instructor's intention either. In order to avoid communication breakdown she chose to change a topic, i.e. to ask a different question. Therefore, Learner 54, not attending to the target-like question forms in the instructor's NF, was neither able to strengthen her interlanguage knowledge nor able to internalize the target-like question forms.

Finally, an interesting finding about the effects of MO is worth considering. That is, the significant effects of MO on EFL question development have been found in the immediate posttest but not in the delayed posttest. In other words, MO is a significant predictor of EFL question development in the immediate posttest whereas not in the delayed posttest. As aforementioned in Chap. 4 there is an interval of two weeks between the two posttests. This finding is supposed to indicate that the effects of MO might not be sustained for a longer period of time. It can also be understood through reference to Levelt's model of speech production (Levelt 1989; Levelt et al. 1999). As indicated by Izumi (2003), the process of output, not language learning per se, can contribute to learning by strengthening the interlanguage knowledge weakly established and not yet internalized. Output may function "as a useful means to promote the interaction between learner internal factors and environmental factors, or the interaction within the learners themselves for internal metalinguistic reflection" (Izumi 2003: 187). Insomuch as modifying output is a cognitive and psycholinguistic process, its effects may be constrained within a short term by learners' internal mechanisms, working memory for instance, when the interlanguage knowledge has not been internalized. Mackey (2006b: 374) pointed out that "results from research studies to date suggest that working memory capacity might be related to the amount and type of benefits that learners gained from oral interaction". Thus, learners with different working memory capacities might benefit differentially from MO in EFL development. The effects of MO on EFL development might be affected by the working memory capacity, which is also expected to be explored in the future research.

5.3.2 Attention and EFL Development

According to the statistical analysis in the present study, the learners' noticing is found significantly predictive of EFL development. This result corroborates the Noticing Hypothesis (Schmidt 1990, 1993, 2001) in a certain aspect. As Schmidt (1990, 1993, 2001), Robinson (2001, 2003) proposed, learners must consciously notice input in order to make it become intake. Alternatively, it is attention, identified as a cognitive process that mediates input and second language development (Gass 1997; Mackey et al. 2000; Philp 2003; Robinson 2001, 2003), that allows learners to notice a gap between what they produce/know and what is produced by their competent interlocutor (Mackey 2006c). Noticing the gap is helpful for input to turn into intake, thus it may promote the target language development. In the study, Learner 54, for example, without reporting attention to question forms, has not advanced to stage 5 in the developmental sequence of question formation, which also confirms the effect of noticing on the interlanguage development.

The significant effect of attention on EFL development is consistent with a series of literature (e.g. Gass 1991, 1997; Mackey 1999; Mackey and Oliver 2002; Philp 1998), about the notable relationship between attention and interlanguage development. The result about the effects of attention, however, is inconsistent with McDonough's (2005) study, in which attention was not found significantly predictive of ESL question development. The discrepancy is interpreted as follows. Compared with McDonough's (2005) study, the distribution of the learners reporting noticing question forms in each treatment group of the two studies is discrepant. As shown in Table 5.1, in the group with an enhanced modification opportunity, the number of the learners reporting noticing question forms (N = 10) is more than that in the other three groups. Nevertheless, in McDonough's (2005) study, no learners in the group without a modification opportunity reported noticing question forms, while 3 learners in each of the other three groups reported noticing question forms. In addition, the types of NF employed in the two studies are different. The NF in the form of recasts and CRs was adopted in the present study, while repetitions and CRs employed in McDonough's (2005) study. Different types of NF may affect the learners' attention to forms, which is supposed to cause the discrepancy between the two studies. This discrepancy also indicates, in some degree, that NF in the form of recasts may arouse the learners' attention to forms more easily in interaction. Therefore, it is necessary to investigate the relationship between the learners' attention and the NF in various forms.

Noticeably, in the group with an enhanced modification opportunity, there were 10 learners reporting noticing question forms. In the other three groups, the number of learners noticing question forms was almost the same, 5, 6, and 6, respectively. This indicates that enhancing the opportunity to modify output can be more likely to arouse the learners' attention to target-like forms in the instructor's feedback. Enhancing the opportunity to modify output is realized by way of recasts followed by CRs in the present study. A recast is firstly provided by the instructor in order to implicitly show target-like forms to the learner. Immediately after the recast, an open-ended CR is then provided to urge the learner to modify his previous output. If the learner can notice the gap between his utterance and the instructor's, he will probably be aware of his error so that he may produce the expected target-like forms in the MO. Such an interactional process may take place repeatedly, during which the learner's interlanguage knowledge can be strengthened, and finally internalized so that the learner may gain in EFL development.

Lastly, an interesting finding about attention is worth taking into account. That is, attention has significant effects on EFL question development in the delayed posttest, but not in the immediate posttest. Alternatively, attention is a significant predictor of EFL question development in the delayed posttest, whereas not in the immediate posttest. It indicates that the role of attention to EFL development may not work immediately after the interactional tasks. This finding can be elucidated in virtue of VanPatten's (1995, 1996) model of Input Processing. The kernel of this model is that human beings possess limited processing capacities. According to Izumi (2003), learners with limited processing capacities firstly search for content words in their more competent interlocutor's NF, as the input. If processing capacities are not exhausted at that time, they may attend to grammatical forms with high communicative value, then grammatical forms with less communicative value on condition that there are still resources left. The construction of stage 5 question is Wh + aux/do, which has little inherent semantic value, so it bears less communicative value. Then, learners may not attend to the construction of stage 5 question in response to the instructor's NF. Additionally, language development derives from intake converted by comprehended input. Gass (1997), Gass and Selinker (1993) claimed that analysis at the level of meaning was not as useful for intake as an analysis made at the level of syntax. In other words, grammatical analysis is more beneficial for input to be converted to intake. Therefore, the benefits of attention to question forms may also be seen after a period of time.

5.3.3 NF and EFL Development

According to Long (1983b), NF is a crucial element of successful foreign/second language instruction. The majority of recent L2 studies have shown the availability of NF in NS-NNS task-based interaction as well as in teacher-student L2 classroom interaction (e.g. Ayoun 2001; Doughty and Varela 1998; Ellis et al. 2006; Iwashita 2003). In the present study the NF in the form of recasts and CRs has been provided to learners in response to their deviant production about questions. The result based on statistical analysis is that the NF employed in the present study has no significant effects on EFL development. The effects of the two types of feedback will be respectively discussed below.

5.3.3.1 Effects of Recasts on EFL Development

As previously stated in Chaps. 2 and 3, the effects of recasts on language development have been in debate for decades. A number of researchers have claimed that recasts are an effective way of providing learners with the differences between their current interlanguage and the target language (Long and Robinson 1998; Nicholas et al. 2001). Some researchers, however, have also argued that a teacher's recast may not be perceived by the learner as NF on the form of their utterance because of the implicitness of recasts (Lyster 1998a; Lyster and Ranta 1997; Panova and Lyster 2002).

The finding on recasts in the present study is that recasts have no significant effects on EFL development. This result may be interpreted by the nature of recasts. A number of researchers have demonstrated that recasts, as a type of NF in interactional processes, are implicit and corrective by nature (e.g., Lyster and Ranta 1997; Long and Robinson 1998; Mackey and Philp 1998). Long and Robinson (1998) placed recasts in the category of implicit negative evidence. Nicholas et al. (2001: 734) noted that "recasts are not explicit, do not isolate the features of language form that are the focus of the feedback, and do not interrupt—even briefly—the flow of meaningful interaction". Obviously, due to its implicitness, recasts do not overtly

5.3 Interaction Process and Foreign Language Development

signal the existence of an error and may not assist in locating the error. Thus, it is not probable for learners to notice the correct forms in recasts. It is also difficult for repair to occur. Consequently, the corrective nature of recasts may not work in promoting language development without learners' attention to correct forms. This has been corroborated by some experimental studies. Lyster (1998b), for instance, has indicated that the levels of repair in uptake following recasts are remarkably lower than those following more explicit types of feedback. In addition, Sheen (2004) has contended that "repair occurred less frequently following recasts than following explicit correction and metalinguistic feedback in four different instruction contexts" (cited from Ellis et al. 2006).

Although in the book statistical analysis has not proved a notable effect of recasts on EFL development, it can not be utterly concluded that recasts do not have any relationship with EFL development. It is supposed that recasts would have an indirect effect on EFL development. The assumption derives from reconsideration about the nature of recasts. Ellis and Sheen (2006) have reexamined the implicitness of recasts. They have pointed out that recasts can also be made explicit. The corrective recasts employed in Doughty and Varela's (1998) study "contained clear signals that made the corrective force of the recast explicit" (cited from Ellis and Sheen 2006: 583). The signals involved the teachers' repetition of the learners' erroneous utterance with stress, and correction with stress. In that case, the correction was made salient to the learners. In other words, the corrective nature of the recasts became more explicit. Thus, Ellis and Sheen (2006: 583) argued that "recasts should not be viewed as necessarily implicit but, rather, depending on the linguistic signals that encode them and the discoursal context, they should be taken as more or less implicit or explicit". Leeman (2000) also suggested that the benefits of recasts might be derived from the enhanced salience of correct forms provided in the recasts. Therefore, the nature of recasts should not be treated as dichotomous on one hand; it may represent a continuum of possibilities ranging from implicitness to explicitness on the other hand. If the corrective nature of recasts can be made more explicit to learners when necessary, it will help learners to notice the correct forms in recasts. Accordingly, the corrective nature of recasts will work in some degree in promoting language development with learners' attention to target-like forms.

5.3.3.2 Effects of CRs on EFL Development

In the study, the significant effects of CRs on EFL development have not been found according to statistical analysis. Nevertheless, CRs, as a type of NF, are supposed to lead to higher rates of modifying output (Anton 1999; Lyster 1998b; Lyster and Ranta 1997). A significant correlation found between CRs and MO in the present study may also support that supposition. As McDonough (2005) noted, CRs may have indirect contribution to EFL development by creating opportunities for learners to modify their output. With Thai EFL learners as subjects, McDonough also pointed out that replication studies involving EFL learners with other cultural and linguistic backgrounds were needed. The result of the present study, with Chinese EFL learners as subjects, is consistent with McDonough's (2005) study. Therefore, the indirect effects of CRs on EFL development have been corroborated again.

The indirect effects of CRs may stem from the learners' different responses to CRs. During the treatment tasks, on the one hand, some learners responded to instructors' CRs by modifying their previous utterances so that the grammatical errors in the previous utterances were corrected or switched to another kind of expression with the same meaning. The modification might help the internalization of target language forms. In other words, such modification might result in more developmentally advanced questions. To put it another way, providing learners with opportunities to modify output by CRs may facilitate language development. On the other hand, other learners responded to instructors' CRs by repeating their previous utterance or changing their previous question to another one. In such a circumstance, these learners were probably not aware of their grammatical errors so as to repeat their utterance. Moreover, they may not know how to correct the errors because the CRs did not provide correct forms so that they could only change to another question form to avoid errors. Hence, it is difficult for these learners to advance to a higher stage in the developmental sequence of question forms.

In addition, since a CR does not comprise target-like forms that the learners need to master, it had better be employed together with a recast which embeds the corresponding positive evidence. Recasts may bring the learners to notice the positive evidence more easily, and then CRs provide the learners enhanced opportunities to modify the deviant parts of their previous utterance. Although no significant difference has been found between the frequencies of MO in the two treatment groups with opportunities to do modification, the combination of recasts and CRs may urge learners to produce MO more frequently. It is supposed to be able to indirectly promote language development. Therefore, more experimental studies about the combination of NF in various forms and its effects on language development are also expected in the future research.

In summary, according to the results of the present study, the NF in the form of recasts and CRs indirectly contribute to EFL development. On the one hand, it can not be predicated absolutely which type of NF employed in the present study is more effective, because either of them can work to promote EFL development in certain conditions. As for recasts, whether this type of NF works in promoting EFL development is related with the explicitness of its corrective nature, and the learners' attention to positive evidence in recasts. As for CRs, the effects of this type of NF on EFL development are related with the learners' awareness of grammatical errors and the learners' proper modification of their output. On the other hand, combining recasts with CRs may be more effective than providing either of them respectively because recasts followed by CRs can enhance the opportunity to modify output. Therefore, during the interactional process the NF in response to the learners' deviant utterance is related with learners' cognitive mechanisms and their output. All these elements jointly function in promoting the learners' EFL development.

5.3.4 Perceptions About NF and EFL Development

The perceptions about NF in interactional processes concern how learners perceive the NF and whether their perceptions have effects on their subsequent EFL development. The present study tries addressing the two issues through task-based dyadic interaction with recasts, CRs, and recasts + CRs as NF. The major findings are listed below.

(1) In this study, the learners' perception about NF can generally be classified into five categories: an error correction, a request for utterance clarification, a guide for task completion, the NF being neglected because of the learners focusing on their tasks, and the interactional episodes being forgotten. Among them, the significant categories involve an error correction, a request for utterance clarification, and a guide for task completion.
(2) Recasts + CRs is more likely to be considered as corrective than CRs. In addition, CR alone is more likely to be regarded as a request for the learners' utterance clarification than recasts or recasts + CRs.
(3) As the significant perception categories, perceiving NF as an error correction, a request for utterance clarification, and a guide for task completion have no significant relationship with EFL development in this experiment.

On the basis of interpreting these findings, we will discuss the characteristics of perceptions about NF in the three treatment groups and its relationship with EFL development in the following two sub-sections.

5.3.4.1 Characteristics of Perceptions About NF

Mackey et al. (2000)'s study has shown that learners are relatively accurate in their perceptions about lexical, semantic, and phonological feedback, whereas syntactic feedback is generally not perceived as such. The present study corroborates their findings about the syntactic feedback. The NF provided to the learners in the study, all related with question formation, belongs to syntactic feedback. The learners did perceive the NF differently, not always as expected. Various characteristics are found in the perceptions about various types of NF in the three treatment groups.

According to the findings of the perception about NF, it is supposed that the perceptions about recasts bear two characteristics. Firstly, recasts are more likely to be perceived as error corrections than other perception categories. This is consistent with some researchers (e.g., Long and Robinson 1998) who have claimed that recasts are effective in showing the differences between the learners' interlanguage and the target language. This is, however, different from the findings from some other researchers (e.g., Lyster and Ranta 1997; Lyster 1998a) who have argued that recasts are ambiguous to learners because recasts may be considered simply as semantic repetitions rather than feedback on forms. Although these studies were conducted under various conditions with various subjects they all found a pair of opposite perceptions about recasts, i.e. error corrections and semantic repetitions. This is also the focus of the current debate.

Secondly, it is under some conditions that recasts are more likely to be perceived as error corrections. One condition is that the learners are not sure about the grammatical forms in their utterances or the learners are aware of their errors in their utterances. In that case, the learners may focus their attention on the teachers' feedback so that it is easy for them to catch the correct forms through feedback. In such a circumstance, the learners may perceive the recasts as error correction. Another condition is that the learners are able to pay attention to correct grammatical forms in the instructors' recasts. For instance, Learner 25 in the second group reported during the stimulated recall period that in the first treatment session, that she did not pay any attention to correct grammatical forms in the instructors' recasts. In the second treatment session, she just paid a little attention to the correct forms. Then, in the third treatment session, she was able to intentionally pay attention to the correct forms. Consequently, according to the stimulated recall data, this learner perceived recasts as error corrections in the second and third treatment sessions. The third condition is when the recasts are short, simple, and involving only one correction, they are easy to be perceived as error correction because of the salience of this correction. This coincides with the result of a study conducted by Egi (2007: 511) who suggested that "length and number of changes in the recasts might, in part, determine the explicitness of recasts as feedback and thus affect learners' abilities to interpret them as such". It is also consistent with the findings in Carpenter et al.'s (2006) study, which indicated that the contrast between a problematic utterance and a recast contributes to learners' interpretations of recasts as corrective.

Meanwhile, the perceptions about CRs are supposed to have three characteristics. Firstly, there is no correct grammatical form embedded in CRs so that this kind of NF is more likely to be perceived as a request for clarifying the utterance. Secondly, under some circumstances CRs can also be perceived as error corrections. That is, when learners are aware that they have encountered grammatical problems in their production of utterances, they may consider CRs as error corrections. Thirdly, the fluency of learners' oral production may affect their perceptions about CRs. When learners can speak fluently during the dyadic interaction, they may be unaware of their grammatical errors but perceive CRs as requests for clarification. For instance, Learner 33 recalled that she did not understand why the teacher wanted her to repeat her fluent utterances. In contrary, when learners can not speak fluently, some of them may correct their errors in response to the teacher's CR, whereas others may not be aware of their grammatical problems and just try to clarify their utterances. For example, Learner 35 recalled that she thought the teacher did not catch her broken utterance so that she just repeated it again. Learner 37 reported that she was aware of her problems in her incoherent utterances and thought that the teacher's CR was a cue for her to correct grammatical errors.

Finally, the perceptions about recasts followed by CRs are supposed to feature in two characteristics. The first one is that in most cases if the learner can notice the teacher's recast, he will regard the following open-ended CR as a hint for him to correct his grammatical mistakes. Take Learner 56 as an example. When he noticed the difference between his utterances and the teacher's utterances he would wake up to his errors and then try to correct the errors after the teacher said "pardon" or "what". The other is that under some conditions the correct forms in teachers' recasts are more likely to be noticed. In other words, when recasts are simple and accord with the learners' original meaning, the correct forms in recasts are easier to notice. Moreover, when the teacher speaks a little slower and the learner is aware of his errors, the correct forms are more likely to be noticed. Otherwise, the learners are more likely to fail to understand the teacher's intention so that they may doubt what to do or just ask a different question.

5.3.4.2 Effects of Perceptions About NF on EFL Development

Few studies have examined whether learners' perception about NF affects their subsequent EFL development through experiments. The present study attempts to do this work. Although we have not found significant effects of perceptions about NF on question development statistically, we believe that the learners' perceptions may have some indirect effects on EFL development. In most cases, when the learners did not perceive the NF as error corrections, they would not develop into stage 5 on the question developmental sequence. On the other hand, when the learners perceived the NF as error corrections, some of them have reached stage 5, while the others have not. Therefore, it indicates that in general the perception about NF as corrective is supposed to be a necessary but insufficient condition for EFL development.

In the second group, the learners were provided with recasts as NF. According to the learners' recall, some of them could notice the correct forms in recasts and they were aware of their errors. However, they did not have opportunities to modify their output. Thus they may not acquire the correct forms. Consequently, they fail to reach stage 5 on the question developmental sequence. In the third group, the learners were provided with CRs as NF. On the basis of the stimulated recall data, some learners in this group are aware of their grammatical errors, but they do not know how to correct them. Hence, they are not likely to reach a higher stage of the question developmental sequence. In the fourth group, the learners were provided with recasts followed by CRs as NF. With the target-like forms available to them, the learners' opportunities to do modification were also enhanced. According to the learners' recall, if they can notice the correct forms in recasts, they will probably modify their output after CRs. Modifying output may subsequently help EFL development. Thus, these learners are likely to reach stage 5 of the question developmental sequence.

Therefore, it can be suggested that the learners' perceptions about NF are related with the nature and the type of the feedback. This coincides with the finding from Mackey et al. (2000)'s study that the nature, as well as the content of the feedback, may have affected learners' perceptions. Meanwhile, the perceptions are also related with the learners' awareness of their grammatical errors. Accordingly, the effects of the learners' perceptions about NF on EFL development are related with the nature and the type of the feedback, their noticing target-like forms in the instructor's NF, and their awareness of their errors. Therefore, the learners' perceptions are supposed to be indirectly related with language development. Whether the learners perceive NF as error corrections might be crucial for its effects on their EFL development. In the future, more experimental studies are desired to investigate the effects of learners' perception on language development, and to establish kind of relationship between learners' perceptions about NF and language development.

5.3.5 Interactional Processes and EFL Development

The present study seeks to answer the paramount question in the interaction field at the moment—how interaction works to bring about positive effects on second/foreign language learning, stated by Mackey and Gass (2006). The results obtained in the present study have gained some insight into the interaction-learning relationship. Long (1996: 451–452) in his update of the Interaction Hypothesis emphasized that "negotiation work that triggers interactional adjustments by the NS or more competent interlocutor, facilitates acquisition because it connects input, internal learner capacities, particularly selective attention, and output in productive way". In the present study, the NF in the form of recasts and CRs is regarded as input. When the learners receive recasts and CRs either respectively or together, they will be provided with different opportunities to modify their output. During the interactional processes, the learners' MO will be affected by the learners' attention to target language forms and their perceptions about the NF provided to them. Accordingly, all these elements are interrelated with each other to facilitate EFL development.

During the interactional processes, how these elements investigated in the present study affect EFL development can also be illustrated on the basis of Gass's (1988) integrated model of SLA because Gass's model provides a detailed description of each component stage and depicts the interrelated and dynamic processes of language acquisition. This model, proposing five stages, i.e. apperceived input, comprehended input, intake, integration, and output, "characterizes what a learner does in moving from exposure to second language input to the production stage of output" (Gass 1997: 2), seen in Fig. 5.1.

Gass claims that learners have to first perceive ambient input in light of their past experiences and currently held knowledge since there is a gap between what the learner already knows and what he is going to know. Apperception is stated as "the process of understanding by which newly observed qualities of an object are initially related to past experiences" (Gass 1997: 4). In the present study, the NF provided by the instructor was considered as a kind of input. If the learner notices the NF in some way because of some particular recognizable features, it may become the apperceived input for further analysis. Therefore, the NF as a hint of the occurrence of grammatical errors may serve as a priming device for learners to conduct later analysis of the input. Nevertheless, not all of the information in NF can be automatically used for comprehension by learners, let alone for intake or integration, or output (Fig. 5.8).

The next stage in Gass's model is comprehended input, referring to the apperceived input that "is processed to derive some form of meaning representation" (Izumi 2003: 172). According to Gass (1997: 5), comprehension here is regarded as "a continuum of possibilities ranging from semantics to detailed structural analyses". In this sense, learners can not only understand the general message but also comprehend the syntactic or phonological pattern presented in the input. In the present study, when the learners comprehend the corrective and structural information of the NF, they may be ready to convert the comprehended input to intake. An indispensable condition for this comprehension to occur is that the learners should notice the corrective and syntactic information embedded in the NF. Noticing the corrective and syntactic information can help learners to detect the gap in their knowledge. Additionally, the learners' perceptions about the apperceived input may also affect their noticing. When the learner perceives the NF as corrective, he will more probably pay attention to the syntactic information. Alternatively, when the learner perceives the NF absolutely as communicative he will more probably neglect the syntactic information.

Subsequently, the comprehended input can feed into the intake stage, which refers to "the mental activity that mediates input and grammars" (Gass 1997: 5). As Izumi (2003) stated, the intake data may be used for the formation of new interlanguage hypotheses. In the book, the comprehension of the corrective and structural information in the NF may help the intake to take place, in which the

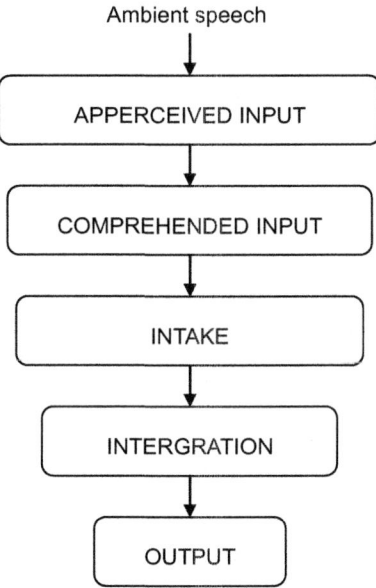

Fig. 5.8 A model of SLA (Gass 1988: 200)

information is matched against the existing internalized grammatical rules about question formation. After that, there comes an integration stage (Gass 1997). If the corrective and structural information in the NF confirms the learner's existing knowledge on question formation, it will facilitate the integration of new question knowledge into the question developmental sequence. If the information is already part of the learner's question knowledge base, it may be used for rule strengthening. If the information contradicts the learner's existing hypothesis, this hypothesis will be rejected. In that case, the learner will search more comprehended input for its conversion into intake.

The final stage is output, which, in one sense, is characterized as an overt manifestation of the acquisition process, and which, in another sense, is also suggested to play active roles in acquisition (Gass 1997). As aforementioned in Chap. 2, Swain (1995) discussed three functions of output, namely, the noticing function, the hypothesis-testing function, and the metalinguistic function. In the present study, as for the noticing function, learners' production of the MO involving stage 5 questions indicates that they may have noticed the corrective and structural information in the NF provided in response to their previous output. This demonstrates that MO is beneficial for noticing the structural information in NF. Thus, this conceptualization of output necessitates a feedback loop to comprehended input. As for the hypothesis-testing function, once learners in the present study produce questions with deviant parts, they received the instructor's NF. Consequently, the learners with opportunities to do modification modified their previous output. Some of them might modify their previous hypothesis by producing stage 5 questions. They may have tested the hypothesis by modifying previous output. Thus, MO may contribute to the intake of new knowledge. As for the metalinguistic function, when the learners in the present study produced MO involving stage 5 questions, the elements of the questions must have been put in some order to fit in with structural rules of EFL question formation. Accordingly, they may first understand its structural rules. Thus, MO may facilitate comprehension of structural information in input and its conversion into intake, thus facilitating its acquisition. Therefore, as Izumi (2003) stated, output generated through the production processes can help to mediate between comprehension and acquisition processes by facilitating noticing of the mismatches between the learners' output and the more competent interlocutor's target language input.

In summary, NF, attention, perception, and MO are interrelated and work together to contribute to second/foreign language development. These components, all indispensable for language development, constitute a continuous process of language development.

Chapter 6
Conclusion and Implications

This chapter will summarize the major findings of the present study and propose implications. Section 6.1 concerns a summary of the major findings in this research. Thereafter, Sect. 6.2 discusses the theoretical, pedagogical, and methodological implications of our study in the book. Finally, Sect. 6.3 addresses the limitations of the study and correspondingly suggests some directions for future research.

6.1 Summary

The book sets out to identify the effects of the NF in the form of recasts and CRs provided by the competent interlocutors, learners' attention and perceptions about the NF and learners' MO in response to the NF on EFL question development, respectively. Besides, it explores how these components are interrelated with each other to facilitate EFL development. A pretest-treatment-posttest research design was employed in the study to investigate all the research questions put forward in Chap. 4. The relevant findings of each research question will be summarized in the following paragraphs.

The first research question is concerned with the effects of the NF in the form of recasts and CRs on EFL question development. As can be seen clearly in the results and discussion reported in Chap. 5, neither recasts nor CRs are found significantly predictive of EFL question development. The NF in the combining form of recasts and CRs, however, may indirectly contribute to EFL question development by distinguishing the corrective nature of the NF for learners to attend to, and by creating opportunities for learners to modify their output. Because NF in the form of recasts may not promote EFL language development without learners' attention to positive evidence in recasts, it is effective to make the corrective nature of recasts more explicit on condition that the communication between the learner and the instructor is ensured. Nevertheless, recasts are supposed to create fewer opportunities for learners to produce MO than CRs (Anton 1999; Linnell 1995; Lyster and

Ranta 1997). The NF in the form of CRs may facilitate EFL development by providing learners with opportunities to modify their output, but this type of NF is not able to provide positive evidence for learners as recasts. Therefore, either recasts or CRs fail to significantly contribute to EFL development, and they have some weaknesses. It is strongly suggested that recasts and CRs be combined as a whole in response to learners' deviant utterances so as to provide positive evidence for them to notice on one hand, and to create enhanced opportunities for learners to modify their previous output on the other hand. In this circumstance, the NF in the form of recasts and CRs may function as indirect factors to facilitate EFL development. Additionally, the function of NF is also related with learners' attention to the target-like forms and the output modification behavior.

The second research question deals with the effect of the learners' MO produced in response to the instructor's NF on EFL question development. The results found in the present study show that the learners do modify their previous output in response to the instructor's NF when there is an opportunity. Some learners can modify their output by producing stage 5 questions, while others just repeat their deviant utterance or change to another topic. The results also indicate that the learners' MO involving stage 5 questions is significantly predictive of EFL question development. The notable effects of MO on EFL question development has been interpreted by reference to Levelt's model of speech production (Levelt 1989; Levelt et al. 1999). As Izumi (2003) suggested, when learners modify their output, they either generate a new message or reprocess their original message, both of which trigger additional grammatical encoding to help learners to strengthen their knowledge representations (Nobuyoshi and Ellis 1993) or encourage automatic retrieval of linguistic forms (de Bot 1996). As a half replication of McDonough's (2005) study, this finding in the present study is also consistent with his study. Additionally the notable effect of MO on EFL question development has been analyzed through the interactional episodes respectively between a learner providing MO with stage 5 questions and an instructor, and a learner without providing MO with stage 5 questions and an instructor. Moreover, there is an interesting finding that MO is a significant predictor of EFL question development in the immediate posttest whereas not in the delayed posttest. This result has been interpreted from the cognitive and psycholinguistic perspective concerning the nature of the process of modifying output. It is suggested that learners' internal mechanisms, such as the working memory capacity, might have some effect on whether the effects of MO will sustain. Thus, we need to conduct more in-depth studies in this field in the future.

The third research question concerns the effect of the learners' noticing question forms on EFL question development in the task-based oral interaction. The results in the present study indicate that the learners' noticing question forms is a significant predictor of EFL question development. This finding contributes to the Noticing Hypothesis (Schmidt 1990, 1993, 2001), and is also consistent with a number of studies (e.g., Gass 1991, 1997; Mackey 1999; Mackey and Oliver 2002; Philp 1998) in the significant relationship between noticing and interlanguage development. This finding, however, contradicts McDonough's (2005) study, in

6.1 Summary

which attention was not found as a significant predictor of ESL question development. The contradiction may stem from the different types of NF employed in the two studies. This contradiction may also indicate that NF in the form of recasts may arouse the learners' attention to the target-like forms more easily during the interactional process in some degree. This supposition needs further studies to address the relationship between the learners' attention to forms and the NF in various forms. Moreover, by the observation of the learners' reporting attention to the question forms in the four treatment groups we may also suggest that enhancing the opportunity to modify output can more probably arouse the learners' attention to the target-like forms, and thereby promote EFL development. Finally, there is a surprising finding that attention is a significant predictor of EFL question development in the delayed posttest, whereas not in the immediate posttest. The delayed role of attention to EFL development has been elucidated on the basis of VanPatten's (1995, 1996) model of Input Processing. That is, during the interactional process, the information about the grammatical form is not easy to notice in the first place, and the analysis made at the level of syntax is more beneficial for input to be converted to intake than the analysis made at the level of meaning (Gass 1997; Gass and Selinker 1993). Therefore, attention to the question forms may not function to facilitate EFL development immediately after interaction takes place.

The fourth research question is concerned with how the learners perceive NF in the form of recasts and CRs and the effect of their perceptions on EFL question development. According to the statistics, the significant categories of the learners' perception involve an error correction, a request for utterance clarification, and a guide for task completion. Recasts followed by CRs are more likely perceived as error correction than CRs, while CRs are more likely regarded as requests for utterance clarification. Another finding is that the learners' perception has no significant relationship with EFL question development. We have tried to summarize the characteristics of the learners' perception about NF in each treatment group. In the treatment group provided with recasts as NF, recasts are more likely to be perceived as corrective under the following three conditions respectively: when the learners are not sure about the grammatical forms in their utterances, or the learners are aware of their errors in their utterances; when the learners are able to pay attention to positive evidence in the instructors' recasts; and when the recasts are short and simple, involving only one correction. In the treatment group provided with CRs as NF, CRs are more likely to be perceived as requests for clarifying the utterance on one hand. When the learners are aware of their grammatical problems, CRs can also be perceived as corrective, on the other hand. Additionally, the fluency of learners' oral production may affect their perceptions about CRs. In the treatment group provided with recasts followed by CRs, if the learner can notice the teacher's recasts, he will regard the following open-ended CR as a hint for him to correct his grammatical errors. Furthermore, the correct forms in recasts are easier to notice when recasts are simple and accord with the learners' original meaning, and when the teacher speaks a little slower and the learner is aware of his errors. After a discussion about the characteristics of the learners' perception about NF in each treatment group, we have also illustrated the indirect effects of perceptions about NF on EFL question development. The indirect effects of the learners' perceptions about NF on EFL question development are related to the nature and the type of the feedback, their noticing target-like forms, and their awareness of their errors. Whether the learners perceive NF as corrective might be crucial for their EFL development.

After discussing each research question, we have tried to expound how these components in the interactional process investigated in the present study are interrelated with each other to facilitate EFL development based on Gass's (1988, 1997) model of SLA. All these components work in a dynamic process with learners' cognitive mechanisms to promote second/foreign language development. Therefore, these components are all indispensable for language development.

6.2 Implications

6.2.1 Theoretical Implications

Though a number of studies contributed to the interaction-learning relationship research, hardly any study has been conducted to provide a systematic analysis of how the components during the interactional process, i.e., NF, MO, attention, and perception, facilitate Chinese EFL learners' question development. The book, trying to fill this important research gap in the literature, can shed light on some relevant theoretical issues of the role of the interaction in second/foreign language production and development.

Firstly, the significant effect of MO on EFL question development provides empirical support for the Output Hypothesis (Swain 1985, 1993, 1995), and coincides with Mackey (1997) and McDonough (2005) on the relationship between MO and ESL question development. This result also reinforces the association between MO and English question development for EFL learners. This implication, however, should be interpreted cautiously. It should be noted that although the result suggests the MO involving developmentally advanced forms be a significant predictor of EFL question development, it does not warrant the proposition that MO is indispensable for language development. Those learners who did not produce MO during the treatment sections in the present study may still advance to a higher stage eventually. Thus, producing MO is supposed to facilitate the language development.

Secondly, the significant effect of attention to question forms on EFL question development provides empirical support for the Noticing Hypothesis (Schmidt 1990, 1993, 2001), strengthens the claim for the relationship between attention and ESL question development during interaction (Mackey 2006a, b, c), and confirms the suggestion for the reliance of SLA research on cognitive science (Tomlin and Gernsbacher 1994). Nevertheless, this implication should also be interpreted cautiously since the finding in the present study does not clearly demonstrate whether

6.2 Implications

the development follows noticing, or is dependent on noticing. As Schmidt (1995: 28) warned, "I am not so sanguine that the Noticing Hypothesis can be proved or disproved … reports of learning without awareness will always flounder" (cited from Mackey 2006c: 423–424). In the present study, some learners reported attention to question forms but they did not advance to a higher stage. In contrary, some learners did not report noticing question forms but they advanced to a higher stage finally. This should be further investigated.

Thirdly, the indirect effects of the NF and the learners' perception about it found in the present study have supported the claims that researchers have made on the interactional benefits for language development (e.g., Gass 1997; Long 1996; Swain 1995). The MO and attention have been found significantly predictive of EFL question development in the present study. Therefore, the NF in the form of recasts and CRs may contribute to EFL question development by creating and enhancing opportunities for learners to modify their output. The learners' perception may also contribute to EFL question development by noticing the target like forms in the NF and perceiving the NF as corrective.

Fourthly, all the results found in the present study provide empirical support for Long's (1996) update of the Interaction Hypothesis. The present study, along with interactionist perspective, attempts to account for how various aspects of the interaction facilitate EFL development. It can be seen that EFL development is promoted through the learners' modified output produced in response to the NF provided by the instructors, noticing target language forms in NF and perceiving the NF as corrective during the interactional process. Moreover, in a recent update of this line of research, Gass and Mackey (2007) argued that it might be time to acknowledge that the term Interaction Hypothesis needs to be reevaluated, due, in particular, to advances in empirical research. They further pointed out that in addition to its designation as a hypothesis, this line of research has also been referred to as the input, interaction, and output model. Therefore, the present study not only has gained insight from this model but also has contributed to this model with Chinese learners' EFL question development as an example in showing how the components during the interactional process, i.e., NF, output, attention and perception, are interacted and interrelated with each other to facilitate EFL development.

Fifthly, the present study reveals that taking various aspects in the interactional process into consideration can provide a better understanding of interaction-learning relationship. On the basis of Gass's (1988, 1997) integrated model of SLA, the present study illustrates how the NF is apperceived and comprehended as useful input, how the useful input is mediated through learners' attention mechanism and converted to intake, how learners produce MO with the integration of new knowledge in response to the NF, and how the MO contributes to the comprehended input and the intake of new knowledge. Thus, the output stage is not the end of language development, but the beginning. This is because the output process can benefit the mediation between comprehension and acquisition processes. The second/foreign language development is a dynamic and continuous process in which every component is regarded as a part of the process. The interaction-learning relationship should be explored dynamically with multiple components being taken into account.

Lastly, the components of the interactional process should not be regarded as dichotomous factors when conducting interaction-learning research. In the present study, for example, the corrective nature of recasts should not be regarded dichotomously as implicit or explicit. According to Ellis and Sheen (2006), recasts can lie at various points on a continuum of linguistic implicitness-explicitness. Doughty and Varela (1998) have stated that the clear signals, such as emphatic stress, contained in corrective recasts made the corrective force of the recast more explicit. In the present study, the instructors have tried to distinguish the corrective nature of recasts by adding CRs after recasts. As a result, most learners have perceived recasts followed by CRs as corrective. The present study has supplemented Doughty and Varela's (1998) study in the finding that the corrective nature of recasts can also be made more explicit by adding some other type of NF, such as, CRs.

6.2.2 Pedagogical Implications

Since the book is concerned with the effects of the NF provided by the competent interlocutors, learners' attention and perceptions about the NF and learners' MO in response to the NF on Chinese EFL learners' question development, it may bring some implications for second/foreign language teaching and learning.

Firstly, it is beneficial that the teacher designs interactional tasks in second/foreign language teaching, especially in teaching the target language forms based on FonF approach (Long 1991). The interactional tasks should be designed in the form of communication, during which the learner's attention is drawn to the target language form for the need of successful communication. Therefore, the interactional tasks overcome the disadvantage of the traditional presentation-practice pedagogy in which grammatical structures are explicitly presented by the teacher in a discrete manner. In other words, each interactional task may be designed with a focus on one grammatical form. Thus, it will be probably easier to make the grammatical form salient to the learners through their communication with the teacher. Moreover, the process of learners' completing the interactional tasks with the teacher might be compatible with the process of SLA proposed by Gass (1988, 1997). Namely, it is advisable that the interactional task be conducted to induce the teacher's interactional feedback and the learner's MO.

Secondly, when completing the interactional task, the teacher may try to provide a variety of appropriate NF in response to the learner's grammatical errors. However, it does not mean that the more NF is provided the better it is for L2/FL learners because excessive feedback may cause learner irritation (McDonough 2005). The NF is used to arouse the learner's attention to the target language form, and to enhance the opportunity for the learner to produce MO. As for recasts, for example, if target language form involved in recasts is made more explicit to the learner by the teacher, the learner may detect the gap between his utterance and the native-like form in the NF. This kind of new knowledge may be integrated into the learner's interlanguage. As for CRs, this kind of NF can be used by the teacher to provide the learner with an opportunity to modify his previous output. Thus, the learner may produce the target language form in MO. Furthermore, the NF may not only take the form of one type of corrective feedback but also employ the combination of two types of corrective feedback. For instance, despite the advantages of recasts and CRs as NF, both of them have disadvantages. Recasts are not as easy as CRs to induce MO, while CRs is not as easy as recasts to draw the learner's attention to the target language form. Therefore, the teacher can combine the two types of NF, i.e., to produce recasts followed by CRs, to draw the learner's attention to target language forms and to enhance the learner's opportunity to modify his output.

Thirdly, the teacher may make use of the output process to facilitate the learner's interlanguage development. To put it another way, the teacher may create opportunities for the learner to produce not only spoken output, but also written output. The activity of producing the target language probably urges second/foreign language learners to consciously recognize some of their linguistic problems, and leads them to notice what they do not know in the target language. Moreover, the activity of producing the target language is a process for the learner to try out new target forms in order to meet communicative needs, during which they may be aware of what does work and what does not. Additionally, the activity of producing the target language may prompt the learner to negotiate about language forms and then strengthen the development of the target language.

Lastly, the learner may not only focus on the semantic aspect during communication, but also try to focus on the syntactic aspect. It is beneficial for the learner to develop his interlanguage system if he is able to focus on the target language form during communication. In that case, the learner may probably practice noticing the target language forms besides meaning during communication. Furthermore, the learner may seize every opportunity to try producing output. The intentional output production practice may help the learner to develop their interlanguage system.

6.2.3 *Methodological Implications*

The present study adopts a pretest-treatment-posttest experimental design to investigate the roles of the NF, learners' attention and perceptions about the NF, and learners' MO in response to the NF in Chinese EFL learners' question development. It may have some methodological implications for gathering introspective data during oral interaction in assessing the learners' perceptions about the NF.

Up to date, there are few studies examining Chinese EFL learners' perceptions about NF during oral interaction by employing introspective verbal report technique. According to Gass and Mackey (2000), stimulated recall methodology, as a kind a retrospective verbal report, can be used to prompt the participants to recall thoughts they had while performing a task or participating in an event. Stimulated recall is a widely used recall technique in interaction studies (e.g., Mackey 2002; Mackey et al. 2000; Mackey and Oliver 2002; Morris and Tarone 2003; Swain and Lapkin 2002). However, this technique is seldom used in the study of Chinese EFL learners' perceptions about NF. In the present study, stimulated recall (Gass and Mackey 2000) was adopted to gather the learners' introspective data on their perceptions about the NF in the form of recasts and CRs. Although stimulated recall technique has been criticized on a number of points, it is still worth employing in interaction-learning research because it can induce the learners' introspective data in the interactional process.

6.3 Limitations and Suggestions for Future Research

Needless to say, despite some contribution to the interaction-learning research, the present study is far from being perfect. Some limitations of the present study are listed below together with the suggestions for the related aspects that deserve to be investigated in the future exploration.

First of all, EFL language development is operationalized very narrowly as the EFL question development. Consequently, it can not be taken for granted that the findings of the study can be generalized for other linguistic features. If more types of linguistic features had been taken into account, more convincing and illuminating results could have been obtained on the effects of the NF, learners' attention and perception about the NF, and MO in response to the NF on EFL development. Thus, in the future research a wide range of linguistic structures should be examined to identify the target language development during the interactional process.

The second limitation is concerned with the type of the NF. Only recasts and CRs were employed as NF in the present study, and it is far from identifying all the effects of NF on EFL development. In the future study other NF types should be investigated to obtain a holistic result about the effect of NF on EFL development.

The third limitation is concerned with the foreign language context where the present study was done. In the present study, all the participants shared the same first language background, namely, Chinese. They shared almost the same amount and way of exposure to English as well. Although the same context may strengthen the internal validity of the study, it may also threaten the external validity in the fact that the results cannot be generalized for the learners in other contexts or from different first language backgrounds. Therefore, replication studies with EFL or ESL learners from a variety of first language background are necessary for the future investigations.

The fourth limitation concerns the time span of the experiments in the present study. Although the significant effects of MO and attention on EFL question development have been shown statistically in the present study, the findings need

6.3 Limitations and Suggestions for Future Research

confirming with longitudinal or more long-term cross-sectional studies. In the present study, the observation of EFL question development only lasted a 7-week period. Thus, all the findings in the present study are tentative. In the future studies, more delayed posttests should be done to offer a better understanding of the target language development during a longer term. Additionally, the longitudinal or more long-term cross-sectional studies may contribute to the question whether the learners who did not immediately gain interlanguage development through treatment can develop their interlanguage system.

The last limitation deals with the methods employed to gather the data on the learners' noticing question forms and their perceptions about the NF in the form of recasts and CRs. In the present study, on one hand, the data about the learners' noticing question forms were gathered through learning journals after each treatment session. Any comments about the question forms in learning journals are regarded as noticing question forms. However, many studies have employed introspective verbal report to assess whether the learners have noticed the target language form. This verbal report protocol will bring more direct information to estimate the learners' noticing. On the other hand, the data about the learners' perceptions about NF in the present study are gathered by way of stimulated recall (Gass and Mackey 2000). With its advantages in inducing the data on the learners' perceptions about the NF, stimulated recall has also been criticized especially "on the memory structures being accessed and on issues of reliability and validity" (Gass and Mackey 2000: 24). Therefore, in the future studies related with the learners' internal mechanisms the introspective verbal report methodologies could be used with full knowledge of its strengths and limitations.

In conclusion, the present study has provided empirical support for the significant effects of MO and the learners' attention on EFL question development, and depicted the indirect effects of the NF and the learners' perceptions about the NF on EFL question development. It also enjoys rich theoretical, pedagogical, and methodological implications. In the future studies, it is suggested that we explore a variety of target language structures and various types of NF among the learners with different first language background by increasingly refined methodology in longitudinal or more long-term cross-sectional investigations in order to gain a more comprehensive picture about the interaction-learning relationship.

Appendix A
Test Items

Name	Topic Discussion	Preparing interviews	Story completion
Examples	Future life; Foreign language learning; Campus life	A person with a high mark in English test in the entrance exam to postgraduate; Bill Gates; The president of your university	A Baby for Nicky; Uncle Harry; A Present for the Queen
Description	Have a discussion with your instructor on the topic	Prepare questions to be used in the oral interviews	Discover a story by asking questions about a series of pictures
Type	Information gap	Information gap	Information gap
Exchange of information	Optional	Optional	Required
Direction of information	Two way	One way	One way

A Baby for Nicky (Pretest)

© Shanghai Jiao Tong University Press and Springer Nature Singapore Pte Ltd. 2018
S. Gu, *Interaction Process and Chinese EFL Learners' Proficiency Development*, https://doi.org/10.1007/978-981-10-6835-5

Appendix A: Test Items

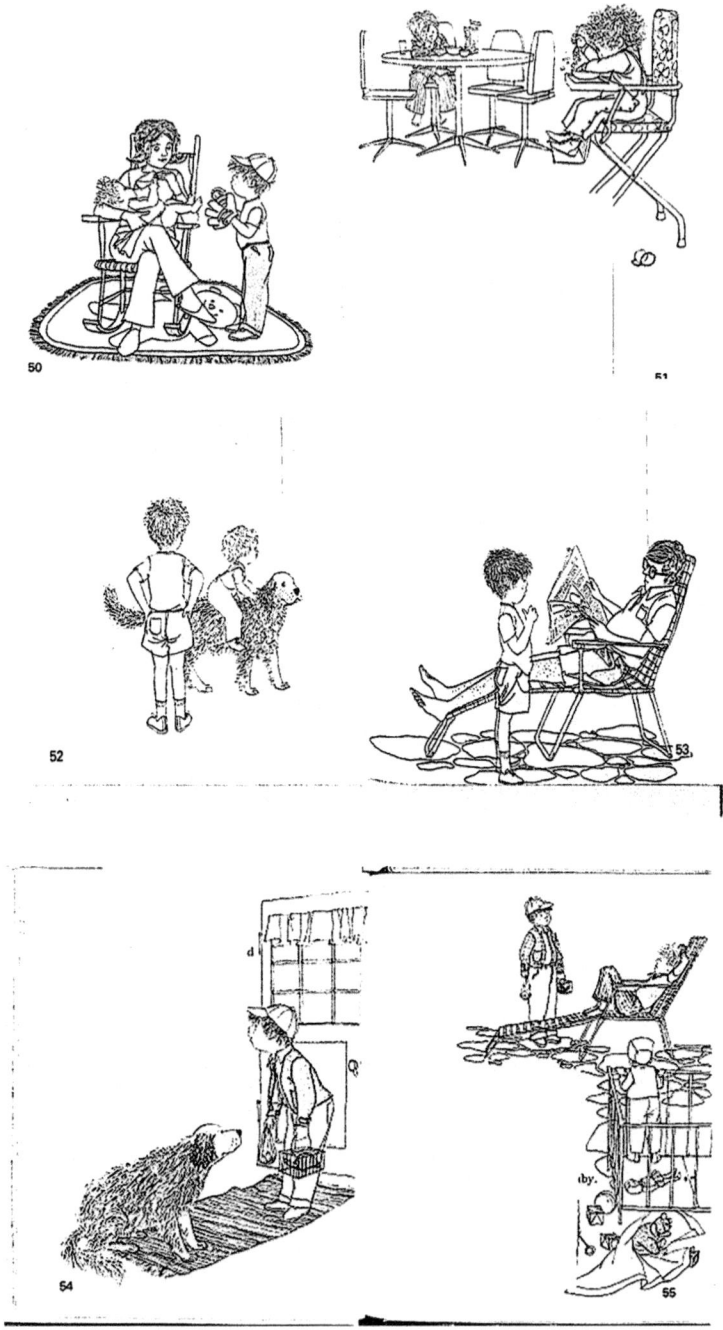

Appendix A: Test Items 125

Uncle Harry (Immediate Posttest)

Appendix A: Test Items

A Present for the Queen (Delayed Posttest)

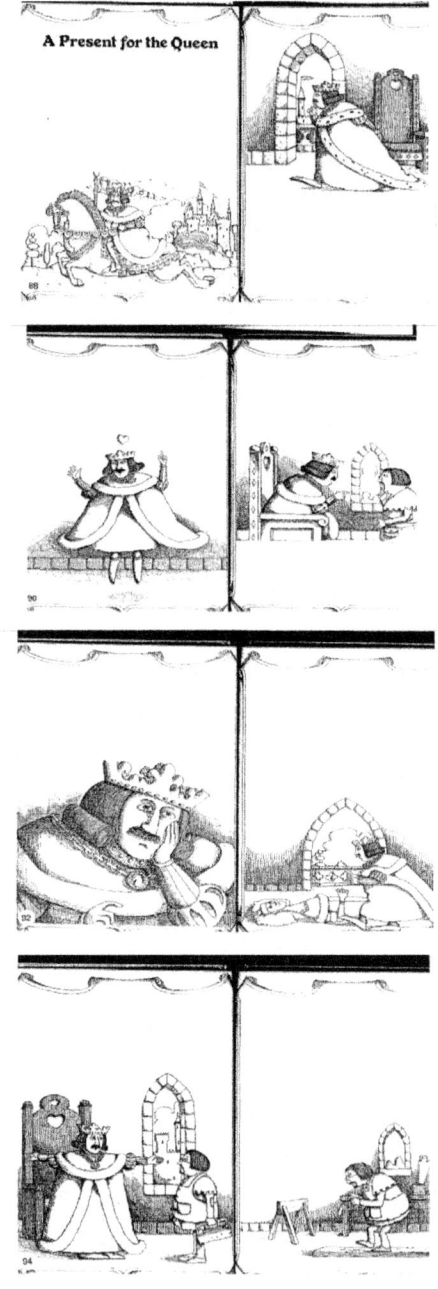

Appendix A: Test Items

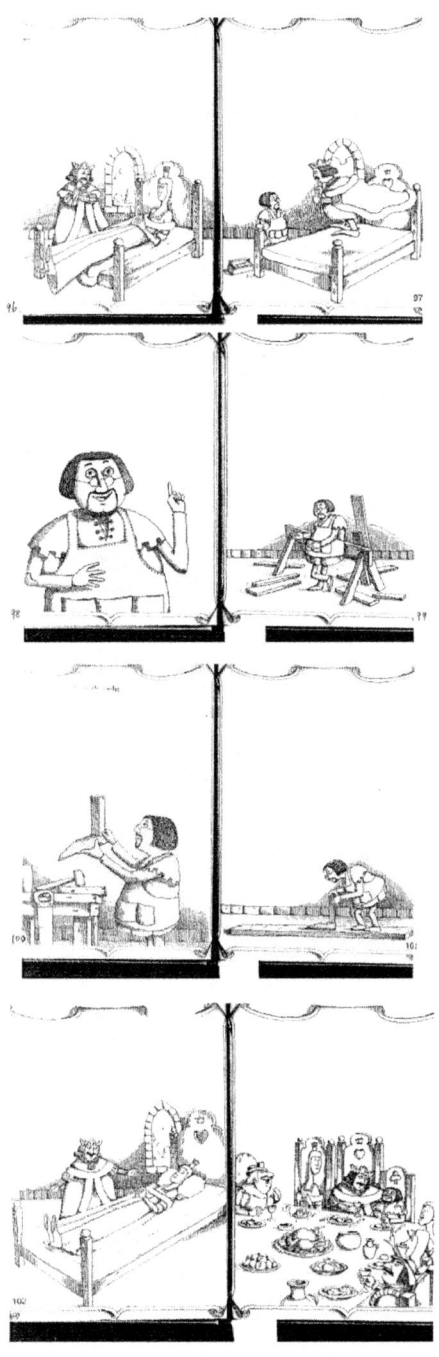

Appendix B
Treatment Activities

Name	Picture differences	Story behind picture	Solving a mystery
Description	Identify differences in two versions of a picture	Find out what happened by asking questions	Discover what the instructor is thinking by asking questions
Type	Information exchange	Information gap	Information gap
Exchange of information	Required	Required	Required
Direction of information	Two way	One way	One way

Picture Differences

Appendix B: Treatment Activities

BOX 53 continued

Picture 2A

Picture 2B

BOX 53 continued

Picture 3A

Picture 3B

Appendix B: Treatment Activities 133

Story behind the Picture

Dialogue pictures

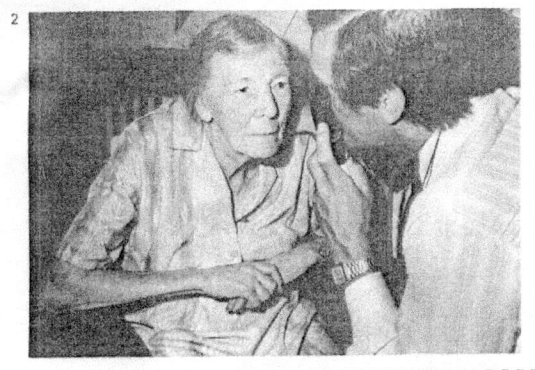

Appendix C
Examples of Developmental Stages and Question Forms

Developmental stages in EFL question formation with data from the present study (stages adapted from Pienemann et al. 1988)

Stages	Constructions	Examples
3. Fronting	Do + SVO?	Do you want to go abroad?
		Do you think it's very hard in the exam?
		*Does they live a happy life?
	Wh + (be/do) SVO?	*Why he frightened?
		*Why the boy is unhappy?
		*Why he want to do?
	Be + SVO?	*Is Nicky let his little brother do that?
		*Are you study English very hard in daily time?
		*Is Nicky helped his little brother at last?
4. Pseudo-inversion; yes/no inversion	(Wh) + copula + S	*What is their hobby?
		*Where is the boy's parents?
		Who are they?
		Are they the boy's father and mother?
	Aux/modal + SV	Can you tell me about how to study English?
		Have you known things about English?
5. Aux second	Wh + aux/do	What kind of exercise do you usually do?
		How long have you studied English?
		What is he doing in this picture?
		How can you do it every day?
		*Why do he always go with the baby?
		*When you are successful what things are you think mostly?
6. Cancelled inversion;	Cancelled inversion	*Have you ever suppose if you don't quit Harvard what your life would be?

(continued)

(continued)

Stages	Constructions	Examples
negative questions; tag questions		*Can you tell us the way how you succeed?
	Negative questions	Why doesn't the girl take it away?
		Why don't you finish school work and choose to do business?
	Tag questions	This is a cat, isn't it?
		*The old man carries it home, isn't it?

Appendix D
Learning Fournal

Did you learn anything today about **Pronunciation**?

Did you learn anything today about **Vocabulary**?

Did you learn anything today about **Grammar**?

Did you learn anything today about **Anything** else?

Appendix E
Questionnaire 1

感谢您的参与，请诚实回答以下问题，这将影响本次研究的结果。

1、年龄 _____ 2、性别 _____

3、专业 _____ 4、母语 _____

5、以前是否学过英语？_____ 如果是，学过几年？_____

6、是否学过其他外语？_____ 如果是，学过几年？_____

  程度如何？_____

7、是否去过说英语的国家？_____ 如果是，待了多久？_____

  去了哪些国家/城市？_____

8、你的父母中有无能说英语或其他外语的？_____

  如果有请详细说明 _____

9、你是否**经常**看英语杂志？_____ **经常**看英语电视电影？_____

  你是否**经常**浏览英语网络？_____ **经常**以其他任何形式接触英语？_____

10、你是否在课外**经常**使用英语？_____

  如果是请举例 _____

11、你学英语的动机包括（可多选）：_____

  1）学校要求

  2）有兴趣

  3）我对以英语为本族语的人和其文化感兴趣

  4）为了专业或事业发展

  5）因为喜欢学习语言

  6）不确定

12、你学英语的动机：_____

  1）非常高　　2）比较高　　3）一般　　4）不太高　　5）没有动机

Appendix F
Exit Questionnaire (Questionnaire 2)

Appendix F: Exit Questionnaire (Questionnaire 2)

性别：_____

组别：_____

1、你认为本次研究对于你的英语问句的习得有无帮助？
1）没有帮助　　　2）有一些帮助　　　3）非常有帮助

2、你认为与你对话的英语教师对于你的英语问句的习得有无帮助？
1）没有帮助　　　2）有一些帮助　　　3）非常有帮助
请具体说明原因：

3、你在参与本次研究之前是否进行过和研究中的交际互动任务形式和内容一样的活动？请分形式和内容两方面举例作答。

4、你认为本次研究中的互动交际任务的目的是什么？对于英语问句的习得有无帮助，在多大程度上有帮助？请举例说明。

5、试验期间，除了与试验中的对话者完成的互动交际任务以外，你是否接触到英语问句训练（比

Appendix F: Exit Questionnaire (Questionnaire 2)

如，在课堂上，或在书本上等）？如果接触了，请注明在何时以及如何接触到的（比如，我学习了一个小时的英语问句；老师在课堂上说明英语问句的提问方法，我们作了练习；我曾在电影里听到了该用法。），并且说明接触到哪些英语问句训练。

6、请写下你对本次研究任何方面的建议或意见。

非常感谢您自始至终参与我们的研究！

请**不要**把本次研究的目的及细节告诉其他人，尤其是其他参与试验但还没有完成互动交际任务测试的同伴，否则从他们那里收集的数据将无法使用。保密对本次研究的顺利完成非常重要。

我明白有关本次研究的任何信息保密的重要性，并不会和参与试验的其他人讨论该研究。

签名：_____
日期：_____

Appendix G
A Consent Form for Participation

研究课题名称: 负反馈、学习者感知及修正后的输出对外语发展的影响
　　课题负责人:　　　顾姗姗　　　电话:(0)13918446909;　　　13775976298
Email: gss@sjtu.edu.cn

　　课题介绍

　　感谢您愿意参加这次研究,本研究将通过口头交流来研究外语学习。 本课题的目的是研究英语学习者如何通过参与交际互动而获益, 参与本研究的被试人员将与资深英语教师共同完成交际任务。 参与本研究时, 被试将有机会积极而有效地使用英语, 并且获得精美礼品。 参与本研究将不会给您造成任何风险和损失。 如有关于参与该课题的任何问题可与课题负责人联系。

　　实验过程

　　研究的试验过程将在六周内完成。 期间,通过第一周的交际互动任务测试, 挑选出符合研究要求的人员作为被试;在接下来的两周内被试人员将同一名英语教师进行三次为时半小时的互动交际任务;第三次任务完成后立即进行交际互动任务测试,两周后再一次测试,整个过程将录像为研究所用。

　　试验数据的保密性

　　有关该研究的任何报告、任何文章或其他任何出版物将严格保密您的个人信息。 在全部数据收集完毕后,研究人员将立即将您的数据编码,并不会透露您的信息给其他人。 录像中的对话部分将被转写成书面文字,方便该课题研究,对话的文字部分有可能会在论文中出现,但决不会透露您的个人信息。 在该课题的后续研究中,您的个人信息也将永远保密。

1、我同意参与此课题研究

我已经阅读该同意书，并愿意参与此课题研究。

签名：_____   日期：_____

2、我同意该数据用于论文或其他相关文章

我已经阅读该同意书，并同意该数据用于论文或其他相关文章。

签名：_____   日期：_____

3、我同意该数据用于该课题后续研究

我已经阅读该同意书，并同意该数据用于该课题后续研究。

签名：_____   日期：_____

4、课题负责人保证该同意书中所述内容真实

签名：_____   日期：_____

Appendix H
Instruction for Stimulated Recall

"刺激回忆"活动说明

你将要听到的是自己和老师完成交际互动任务的录音片段。你在收听时，录音会被暂停若干次，当暂停时，请用汉语告诉老师<u>在完成互动任务的</u><u>当时</u>你想到了什么，感觉到了什么，请注意<u>不是现在</u>所想的。如果你收听时想针对听到的某些片断说些什么，也可以让老师暂停录像。

关于你所想到的东西没有对错而言。你的回忆可以关于任何方面，比如关于声音、关于语言、关于进行的任务，或别的什么。你的回答根据实际可长可短，如果真的不记得当时所想，或者真的没有想什么，也可直说。期间，不要向老师询问有关该研究的问题。

References

Adams, R. 2003. L2 output, reformulation and noticing: Implications for IL development. *Language Teaching Research* 2: 347–376.

Al-Hejin, B. 2004. Attention and awareness: Evidence from cognitive and second language acquisition research. *Working Papers in TESOL & Applied Linguistics* 4: 1–22.

Allwright, D. 1975. Problems in the study of the language teacher's treatment of learner error. In *New Directions in Second Language Learning, Teaching and Bilingual Education: On TESOL'75*, ed. M. Burt, and H. Dulay, 96–109. Washington: TESOL.

Allwright, D., and K. Bailey. 1991. *Focus on the language classroom*. Cambridge: Cambridge University Press.

Anderson, R. (ed.). 1983. *Second Languages: A cross-linguistic perspective*. Rowley, MA: Newbury House.

Anton, M. 1999. The discourse of a learner-centered classroom: Sociocultural perspectives on teacher-learner interaction in the second-language classroom. *Modern Language Journal* 83: 303–318.

Ayoun, D. 2001. The role of negative and positive feedback in the second language acquisition of the *passé composé* and *imparfait*. *The Modern Language Journal* 85: 226–243.

Bearden, R.J. 2003. *Chatting in a Foreign Language: An interactional study of Spanish oral versus computer-assisted discussion in native speaker and non-native learner dyads*. Doctoral dissertation, University of Texas, Austin.

Beck, M., and L. Eubank. 1991. Acquisition theory and experimental design: A critique of Tomasello and Herron. *Studies in Second Language Acquisition* 13: 73–76.

Bell-Corrales, M. 2001. *The Role of Negative Feedback in Second Language Instruction*. Doctoral dissertation, University of Florida, Florida.

Bley-Vroman, R. 1990. The logical problem of foreign language learning. *Linguistic Analysis* 20: 3–49.

Braidi, S. 2002. Reexamining the role of recasts in native-speaker/nonnative-speaker interactions. *Language Learning* 52: 1–42.

Braine, M.D.S. 1994. Is nativism sufficient? *Journal of Child Language* 21: 9–31.

Bygate, M. 2001. Effects of task repetition on the structure and control of oral language. In *Researching Pedagogic Tasks: Second Language Learning, Teaching, and Testing*, ed. M. Bygate, P. Skehan, and M. Swain, 23–48. Pearson Education: Harlow.

Calvé, P. 1992. Corriger ou ne pas corriger, là n'est pas la question. *The Canadian Modern Language Review* 48: 458–471.

Carpenter, H., K. Jeon, D. MacGregor, and A. Mackey. 2006. Learners' interpretations of recasts. *Studies in Second Language Acquisition* 28: 209–236.

Chaudron, C. 1977. A descriptive model of discourse in the corrective treatment of learners' errors. *Language Learning* 26: 45–66.

Chaudron, C. 1986. Teachers' priorities in correcting learners' errors in French immersion classes. In *Talking to Learn: Conversation in Second Language Acquisition*, ed. R. Day, 64–84. Rowley, MA: Newbury House.

Chaudron, C. 1987. The role of error correction in second language teaching. In *Patterns of Classroom Interaction in Southeast Asia*, ed. B. Das, 17–50. Singapore: SEAMEO Regional Language Centre.

Chaudron, C. 1988. *Second Language Classrooms*. Cambridge: Cambridge University Press.

Child, D. 1981. *Psychology and the Teacher*. East Sussex: Holt, Rinehart and Winston Ltd.

Chomsky, N. 1981. *Lectures on Government and Binding*. Dordrecht: Foris.

Chuanhua, Yu. 2007. *SPSS and Statistical Analysis*. Beijing: Publishing House of Electronics Industry.

Chun, A., R. Day, N. Chenoweth, and S. Luppescu. 1982. Errors, interaction, and corrections: A study of native-nonnative conversations. *TESOL Quarterly* 16: 537–546.

Cook, V. 1993. *Linguistics and Second Language Acquisition*. New York: St. Martin's Press.

Corder, S. 1967. The significance of learners' errors. *International Review of Applied Linguistics* 4: 161–170.

Day, R., N. Chenoweth, A. Chun, and S. Luppescu. 1984. Corrective feedback in native-nonnative discourse. *Language Learning* 34: 19–45.

de Bot, K. 1996. The psycholinguistics of the output hypothesis. *Language Learning* 46: 529–555.

de Bot, K., T. Paribakht, and M. Wesche. 1997. Toward a lexical processing model for the study of second language vocabulary acquisition: Evidence from ESL reading. *Studies in Second Language Acquisition*. 19: 309–329.

DeKeyser, R. 2005. What makes learning second-language grammar difficult? A review of issues55. *Language Learning* 55 (Supplement 1): 1–25.

DeKeyser, R., and K. Sokalski. 1996. The differential role of comprehension and production practice. *Language Learning* 46: 613–642.

Doughty, C. 1994. Fine tuning of feedback by competent speakers to language learners. In *Georgetown University Round Table (GURT) 1993*, ed. J. Alatis, 96–108. Washington, DC: Georgetown University Press.

Doughty, C. 1999. The cognitive underpinnings of focus on form. *University of Hawaii Working Papers in ESL* 18: 1–69.

Doughty, C., and E. Varela. 1998. Communicative focus on form. In *Focus on Form in Classroom Second Language Acquisition*, ed. C. Doughty, and J. Williams, 114–138. Cambridge: Cambridge University Press.

Doughty, C., and J. Williams. 1998. Pedagogical choices in focus on form. In *Focus on form in classroom second language acquisition*, ed. C. Doughty, and J. Williams, 197–261. Cambridge: Cambridge University Press.

Egi, T. 2002, April. *Recasts, Noticing and L2 Development during Oral Interaction*. Paper presented at the AAAL 2002, Salt Lake City, UT.

Egi, T. 2004. *Recasts, Perceptions, and L2 Development*. Doctoral dissertation, Georgetown University, Washington, DC.

Egi, T. 2007. Interpreting recasts as linguistic evidence: The roles of linguistic target, length, and degree of change. *Studies in Second Language Acquisition* 29: 511–537.

Ellis, R. 1985. Teacher-pupil interaction in second language development. In *Input in Second Language Acquisition*, ed. S. Gass, and C. Madden, 69–85. Rowley, MA: Newbury House.

Ellis, R. 1994. *The Study of Second Language Acquisition*. Shanghai: Shanghai Foreign Language Education Press.

Ellis, R. 1995. Interpretation tasks for grammar teaching. *TESOL Quarterly* 29: 87–105.

Ellis, R. 2001. Introduction: Investigating form-focused instruction. *Language Learning* 51 (Supplement): 1–46.

Ellis, R. 2007. *Corrective Feedback in Theory, Research and Practice*. Paper presented at The 5th International Conference on ELT in China & the 1st Congress of Chinese Applied Linguistics. Beijing, China.

Ellis, R., H. Basturkmen, and S. Loewen. 2001. Learner uptake in communicative ESL lessons. *Language Learning* 51: 281–318.
Ellis, R., H. Basturkmen, and S. Loewen. 2002. Doing focus-on-form. *System* 30: 419–432.
Ellis, R., and X. He. 1999. The roles of modified input and output in the incidental acquisition of word meanings. *Studies in Second Language Acquisition.* 21: 285–301.
Ellis, R., S. Loewen, and R. Elam. 2006. Implicit and explicit corrective feedback and the acquisition of L2 grammar. *Studies in Second Language Acquisition* 28: 339–368.
Ellis, R., and Y. Sheen. 2006. Reexamining the role of recasts in second language acquisition. *Studies in Second Language Acquisition* 28: 575–600.
Fotos, S. 1998. Shifting the focus from forms to form in the EFL classroom. *ELT Journal* 52: 301–307.
Gass, S. 1988. Integrating research areas: A framework for second language studies. *Applied Linguistics* 9: 198–217.
Gass, S. 1990. Second and foreign language learning: Same, different or none of the above? In *Second Language Acquisition/Foreign Language Learning*, ed. B. VanPatten, and J.F. Lee, 34–44. Clevedon: Multilingual Matters Ltd.
Gass, S. 1991. Grammar instruction, selective attention and learning process. In *Foreign/Second Language Pedagogy Research*, ed. R. Phillipson, E. Kellerman, L. Selinker, M. Sharwood Smith, and M. Swain, 134–141. Clevedon, UK: Multilingual Matters.
Gass, S. 1997. *Input, Interaction, and the Second Language Learner*. Mahwah. NJ: Lawrence Erlbaum Associates.
Gass, S. 2003. Input and interaction. In *Handbook of Second Language Acquisition*, ed. C. Doughty, and M. Long, 224–255. Oxford: Blackwell Publishers.
Gass, S., and A. Mackey. 2000. *Stimulated Recall Methodology in Second Language Research*. Mahwah, NJ: Lawrence Erlbaum Associates, Inc., Publishers.
Gass, S., and A. Mackey. 2007. Input, interaction and output in SLA. In *Theories in SLA*, ed. B. VanPatten, and J. Williams. Mahwah, NJ: Erlbaum.
Gass, S., A. Mackey, and T. Pica. 1998. The role of input and interaction in second language acquisition: An introduction. *Modern Language Journal* 82: 299–307.
Gass, S., and L. Selinker. 1993. *Second Language Acquisition: An introductory course*. Mahwah, NJ: Lawrence Erlbaum Associates.
Gass, S., and E. Varonis. 1989. Incorporated repairs in NNS discourse. In *The Dynamic Interlanguage*, ed. M. Eisenstein, 71–86. New York: Plenum.
Gass, S., and E. Varonis. 1994. Input, interaction, and second language production. *Studies in Second Language Acquisition* 16: 283–302.
Gleason, J. 2005. *The Development of Language*. Beijing: World Publishing Corporation.
Grimshaw, J., and S. Pinker. 1989. Positive and negative evidence in language acquisition. *Behavioral and Brain Sciences* 12: 341–342.
Han, Z. 2002. A study of the impact of recasts on tense consistency in L2 output. *TESOL Quarterly* 36: 543–572.
Hatch, E. 1978. Acquisition of syntax in a second language. In *Understanding Second and Foreign Language Learning*, ed. J. Richards, 34–70. Rowley, MA: Newbury House.
Havranek, G. 2002. When is corrective feedback most likely to succeed? *International Journal of Educational Research* 37: 255–270.
Hendrickson, J. 1978. Error correction in foreign language teaching: Recent theory, research, and practice. *Modern Language Journal* 62: 387–398.
Hwang, J. 1999. *Attention and Second Language Acquisition: The role of detection in the L2 acquisition of English passives*. Doctoral dissertation, University of Oregon, Eugene, OR.
Iwashita, N. 2003. Negative feedback and positive evidence in task-based interaction. *Studies in Second Language Acquisition* 25: 1–36.
Izumi, S. 2002. Output, input enhancement and the noticing hypothesis: An experimental study on ESL relativization. *Studies in Second Language Acquisition* 24: 541–577.

Izumi, S. 2003. Comprehension and production processes in second language learning: In search of the psycholinguistic rationale of the output hypothesis. *Applied Linguistics* 24: 168–196.
Kormos, J. 1999. The effect of speaker variables on the self-correction behavior of L2 learners. *System* 27: 207–221.
Krashen, S. 1985. *The Input Hypothesis: Issues and implications.* London: Longman.
Kui, Lin. 2006. *A Study of the Effects of Recasts on Learners' L2 Output—On subject-predicate agreement of present simple tense of the third person singular.* Ph.D. Dissertation of Guangdong University of Foreign Studies. www.cnki.net.
Leeman, J. 2000. *Towards a New Classification of Input: An empirical study of the effect of recasts, negative evidence and enhanced salience on L2 development.* Doctoral dissertation, Georgetown University, Washington, DC.
Leeman, J. 2003. Recasts and second language development: Beyond negative evidence. *Studies in Second Language Acquisition* 25: 37–63.
Leow, R. 1998. Toward operationalizing the process of attention in SLA: Evidence for Tomlin & Villa's (1994) fine-grained analysis of attention. *Applied Psycholinguistics* 19: 133–159.
Leow, R. 2001. Attention, awareness, and foreign language behavior. *Language Learning* 51: 113–155.
Leow, R. 2002. Models, attention, and awareness in SLA: A response to Simard and Wong's "Alertness, orientation, and detection: The conceptualization of attention functions in SLA". *Studies in Second Language Acquisition* 24: 113–119.
Leow, R.P., and K. Morgan-Short. 2004. To think aloud or not to think aloud: The issue of reactivity in SLA research methodology. *Studies in Second Language Acquisition* 26: 35–57.
Levelt, W. 1978. Skill theory and language teaching. *Studies in Second Language Acquisition* 1: 53–70.
Levelt, W. 1989. *Speaking: From intention to articulation.* Cambridge, MA: The MIT Press.
Levelt, W., A. Roelofs, and A. Meyer. 1999. A theory of lexical access in speech production. *Behavioral and Brain Sciences* 22: 1–75.
Lightbown, P. 1998. The importance of timing in focus on form. In *Focus on Form in Classroom Second Language Acquisition,* ed. C. Doughty, and J. Williams, 177–196. Cambridge: Cambridge University Press.
Lightbown, P. 2000. Anniversary article: Classroom SLA research and second language teaching. *Applied Linguistics* 21: 431–462.
Lin, Y., and J. Hedgcock. 1996. Negative feedback incorporation among high-proficiency and low proficiency Chinese speaking learners of Spanish. *Language Learning* 46: 567–611.
Linnell, J. 1995. Can negotiation provide a context for learning syntax in a second language? *Working Papers in Educational Linguistics* 11: 83–103.
Loewen, S. 2005. Incidental focus on form and second language learning. *Studies in Second Language Acquisition* 27: 361–386.
Long, M. 1983. Linguistic and conversational adjustments to nonnative speakers. *Studies in Second Language Acquisition* 5: 177–194.
Long, M. 1983. Native speaker/non-native speaker conversation and the negotiation of comprehensible input. *Applied Linguistics* 4: 177–193.
Long, M. 1985. Input and second language acquisition theory. In *Input in Second Language Acquisition,* ed. S. Gass, and C. Madden, 377–393. Rowley, MA: Newbury House.
Long, M. 1991. Focus on form: A design feature in language teaching methodology. In *Foreign Language Research in Cross-cultural Perspective,* ed. K. DeBot, R. Ginsberg, and C. Kramsch, 39–52. Amsteram: Benjamins.
Long, M. 1996. The role of the linguistic environment in second language acquisition. In *Handbook of Research on Language Acquisition: Vol. 2. Second Language Acquisition,* ed. W. C. Ritchie, and T.K. Bhatia, 413–468. San Diego, CA: Academic Press.
Long, M., S. Inagaki, and L. Ortega. 1998. The role of implicit negative feedback in SLA: Models and recasts in Japanese and Spanish. *Modern Language Journal* 82: 357–371.

References

Long, M., and P. Robinson. 1998. Focus on form: Theory, research and practice. In *Focus on Form in Classroom Second Language Acquisition*, ed. C. Doughty, and J. Williams, 15–41. Cambridge: Cambridge University Press.

Lyster, R. 1998. Recasts, repetition, and ambiguity in L2 classroom discourse. *Studies in Second Language Acquisition* 20: 51–92.

Lyster, R. 1998. Negotiation of forms, recasts, and explicit correction in relation to error types and learner repair in immersion classrooms. *Language Learning* 48: 183–218.

Lyster, R. 2004. Differential effects of prompts and recasts in form-focused instruction. *Studies in Second Language Acquisition* 26: 399–432.

Lyster, R., and L. Ranta. 1997. Corrective feedback and learner uptake. *Studies in Second Language Acquisition* 19: 37–66.

Mackey, A. 1999. Input, interaction, and second language development: An empirical study of question formation in ESL. *Studies in Second Language Acquisition* 21: 557–587.

Mackey, A. 2002. Beyond production: Learners' perceptions about interactional processes. *International Journal of Educational Research* 37: 379–394.

Mackey, A. 2006a. *Research on Cognition and Interaction in SLA*. Paper presented at the workshop in Georgetown University, Washington, DC.

Mackey, A. 2006b. Epilogue. From introspections, brain scans, and memory tests to the role of social context: Advancing research on interaction. *Studies in Second Language Acquisition* 28: 369-379.

Mackey, A. 2006. Feedback, noticing and instructed second language learning. *Applied Linguistics* 27: 405–430.

Mackey, A., and S. Gass. 2006. Introduction. *Studies in Second Language Acquisition* 28: 169–178.

Mackey, A., S. Gass, and K. McDonough. 2000. How do learners perceive interactional feedback? *Studies in Second Language Acquisition* 22: 471–497.

Mackey, A., and R. Oliver. 2002. Interactional feedback and children's L2 development. *System* 30: 459–477.

Mackey, A., R. Oliver, and J. Leeman. 2003. Interactional input and the incorporation of feedback: An exploration of NS-NNS and NNS-NNS adult and child dyads. *Language Learning* 53: 35–66.

Mackey, A., R. Oliver, and J. Philp. 1997. *The Provision and Use of INF in NNS-NNS Conversation*. Paper presented at Second Language Research Forum.

Mackey, A., and J. Philp. 1998. Conversational interaction and second language development: Recasts, responses, and red herrings? *The Modern Language Journal* 82: 338–356.

Mackey, A., J. Philp, T. Egi, A. Fujii, and T. Tatsumi. 2002. Individual differences in working memory, noticing of interactional feedback and L2 development. In *Individual Differences and Instructed Language Learning*, ed. P. Robinson, 181–209. Philadelphia: John Benjamins.

Marcus, G. 1993. Negative evidence in language acquisition. *Cognition* 46: 53–85.

McDonough, K. 2005. Identifying the impact of negative feedback and learners' responses on ESL question development. *Studies in Second Language Acquisition* 27: 79–103.

McDonough, K., and A. Mackey. 2006. Responses to recasts: Repetitions, primed production, and linguistic development. *Language Learning* 56: 693–720.

McLaughlin, B. 1987. *Theories of Second Language Learning*. London: Edward Arnold.

Ming, Sun, Zhao Fei, and Zhao Jiangkui. 2007. A Study of the Roles of Interactive Feedback on L2 Children's Development of Question Forms. *Foreign Language Teaching*. 2: 1–15.

Morris, F. 2002. *Learner-learner Interaction in the Spanish Foreign Language Classroom: The effects of recasts and negotiation on L2 development*. Doctoral dissertation, University of Minnesota, Minneapolis, MN.

Morris, F., and E. Tarone. 2003. Impact of classroom dynamics on the effectiveness of recasts in second language acquisition. *Language Learning* 53: 325–368.

Muranoi, H. 1996. *Effects of Interaction Enhancement on Restructuring of Interlanguage grammar: A cognitive approach to foreign language instruction.* Doctoral dissertation, Georgetown University, Washington, DC.

Nabei, T., and M. Swain. 2002. Learner awareness of recasts in classroom interaction: A case study of an adult EFL student's second language learning. *Language Awareness* 11: 43–63.

Nassaji, H. 1999. Towards integrating form-focused instruction and communicative interaction in the second language classroom: Some pedagogical possibilities. *The Canadian Modern Language Review* 55: 385–402.

Nassaji, H., and S. Fotos. 2004. Current developments in research on the teaching of grammar. *Annual Review of Applied Linguistics* 24: 126–145.

Nicholas, H., P. Lightbown, and N. Spada. 2001. Recasts as feedback to language learners. *Language Learning* 51: 719–758.

Nobuyoshi, J., and R. Ellis. 1993. Focused communication tasks and second language acquisition. *ELT Journal* 47: 203–210.

Norris, J., and L. Ortega. 2000. Effectiveness of L2 instruction: A research synthesis and quantitative meta-analysis. *Language Learning* 50: 417–528.

O'Grady, W. 1996. Language acquisition without Universal Grammar: A general nativist proposal for L2 learning. *Second Language Research* 12: 374–397.

Oliver, R. 1995. Negative feedback in child NS/NNS conversation. *Studies in Second Language Acquisition* 18: 59–481.

Oliver, R. 1998. Negotiation of meaning in child interactions. *Modern Language Journal* 82: 372–386.

Oliver, R. 2000. Age differences in negotiation and feedback in classroom and pairwork. *Language Learning* 50: 119–151.

Oliver, R., and A. Mackey. 2003. Interactional context and feedback in child ESL classrooms. *Modern Language Journal* 87: 519–533.

Ortega, L., and M. Long. 1997. The effects of models and recasts on the acquisition of object topicalization and adverb placement in L2 Spanish. *Spanish Applied Linguistics* 1: 65–86.

Panova, I., and R. Lyster. 2002. Patterns of corrective feedback and uptake in an adult ESL classroom. *TESOL Quarterly* 36: 573–595.

Philp, J. 1998. *Interaction, Noticing, and Second Language Acquisition: An examination of learners' noticing of recasts in task-based interaction.* Doctoral dissertation, University of Tasmania, Australia.

Philp, J. 2003. Constraints on "noticing the gap": Nonnative speakers' noticing of recasts in NS-NNS interaction. *Studies in Second Language Acquisition* 25: 99–126.

Pica, T. 1988. Interlanguage adjustments as an outcome of NS-NNS negotiated interaction. *Language Learning* 38: 45–73.

Pica, T. 1992. The textual outcomes of native speaker-non-native speaker negotiation: What do they reveal about second language learning? In *Text and Context: Cross-disciplinary Perspectives on Language Study*, ed. C. Kramsch, and S. McConnell-Ginet, 198–237. Lexington MA: D. C. Heath.

Pica, T. 1994. Research on negotiation: What does it reveal about second-language learning conditions, processes, and outcomes? *Language Learning* 44: 493–527.

Pica, T., L. Holliday, N. Lewis, and L. Morgenthaler. 1989. Comprehensible output as an outcome of linguistic demands on the learner. *Studies in Second Language Acquisition* 11: 63–90.

Pienemann, M., M. Johnston, and G. Brindley. 1988. Constructing an acquisition-based procedure for second language assessment. *Studies in Second Language Acquisition* 10: 217–243.

Robinson, P. 1995. Attention, memory and the "noticing" hypothesis. *Language Learning* 45: 283–331.

Robinson, P. 2001. Individual differences, cognitive abilities, aptitude complexes and learning conditions in second language acquisition. *Second Language Research* 17: 368–392.

Robinson, P. 2003. Attention and memory during SLA. In *Handbook of Second Language Acquisition*, ed. C. Doughty, and M. Long, 631–678. Oxford: Blackwell Publishing.

Saito, H. 1999. Dependence and interaction in frequency data analysis in SLA research. *Studies in Second Language Acquisition* 21: 453–475.
Saxton, M. 1997. The contrast theory of negative input. *Journal of Child Language* 24: 139–161.
Schachter, J. 1991. Corrective feedback in historical perspective. *Second Language Research* 7: 89–102.
Schachter, J. 1998. Recent research in language learning studies: Promises and problems. *Language Learning* 48: 557–583.
Schmidt, R. 1990. The role of consciousness in second language learning. *Applied Linguistics* 11: 129–158.
Schmidt, R. 1993. Awareness and second language acquisition. *Annual Review of Applied Linguistics* 13: 206–226.
Schmidt, R. 1994. Deconstructing consciousness in search of useful definitions for applied linguistics. *AILA Review* 11: 11–26.
Schmidt, R. 1994. Implicit learning and the cognitive unconscious: Of artificial grammars and SLA. In *Implicit and Explicit Learning of Languages*, ed. N. Ellis, 165–209. San Diego, CA: Academic Press.
Schmidt, R. 1995. Consciousness and foreign language learning: A tutorial on the role of attention and awareness in learning. In *Attention and Awareness in Foreign Language Learning*, ed. R. Schmidt, 1–63. Honolulu: University of Hawaii, Second Language Teaching and Curriculum Center.
Schmidt, R. 2001. Attention. In *Cognition and Second Language Instruction*, ed. P. Robinson, 3–32. Cambridge: Cambridge University Press. Rpt. Beijing: World Publishing Corporation, 2007.
Schmidt, R., and S. Frota. 1986. Developing basic conversational ability in a second language: A case study of an adult learner of Portuguese. In *Talking to Learn: Conversation in Second Language Acquisition*, ed. R. Day, 237–326. Rowley, MA: Newbury House.
Schwartz, B. 1993. On explicit and negative data effecting and affecting competence and linguistic behavior. *Studies in Second Language Acquisition* 15: 147–163.
Sheen, R. 2003. Focus on form-a myth in the making? *ELT Journal* 57 (3): 225–233.
Smith, C., and V. Arnold. 1986. *Rainbow World*. NY: Macmillan Publishing Company.
Spada, N., and P. Lightbown. 1993. Instruction and the development of questions in L2 classrooms. *Studies in Second Language Acquisition* 15: 205–224.
Swain, M. 1985. Communicative competence: Some roles of comprehensible input and comprehensible output in its development. In *Input in Second Language Acquisition*, ed. S. Gass, and C. Madden, 235–253. Rowley, MA: Newbury House.
Swain, M. 1993. The output hypothesis: Just speaking and writing aren't enough. *The Canadian Modern Language Review* 50: 158–164.
Swain, M. 1995. Three functions of output in second language learning. In *For H. G. Widdowson: Principles and Practice in the Study of Language*, ed. G. Cook, and B. Seidhofer, 125–144. Oxford: Oxford University Press.
Swain, M. 1998. Focus on form through conscious reflection. In *Focus on Form in Classroom Second Language Acquisition*, ed. C. Doughty, and J. Williams, 64–81. Cambridge: Cambridge University Press.
Swain, M. 2007. *The Output Hypothesis: Its history and its future*. Paper presented at The 5th International Conference on ELT in China & the 1st Congress of Chinese Applied Linguistics. Beijing, China.
Swain, M., and S. Lapkin. 1995. Problems in output and the cognitive processes they generate: A step towards second language learning. *Applied Linguistics* 16: 371–391.
Swain, M., and S. Lapkin. 2002. Talking it through: Two French immersion learners' response to reformulation. *International Journal of Educational Research* 37: 285–304.
Tomasello, M., and C. Herron. 1988. Down the garden path: inducing and correcting overgeneralization errors in the foreign language classroom. *Applied Psycholinguistics* 9: 237–246.

Tomasello, M., and C. Herron. 1989. Feedback for language transfer errors: the garden path technique. *Studies in Second Language Acquisition* 11: 385–395.
Tomlin, R., and M. Gernsbacher. 1994. Cognitive foundations of second language acquisition. *Studies in Second Language Acquisition* 16: 129–132.
Tomlin, R., and V. Villa. 1994. Attention in cognitive science and second language acquisition. *Studies in Second Language Acquisition* 16: 183–202.
Trahey, M., and L. White. 1993. Positive evidence and preemption in the second language classroom. *Studies in Second Language Acquisition* 15: 181–203.
Truscott, J. 1998. Noticing in second language acquisition: A critical review. *Second Language Research* 14: 103–135.
Ur, P. 1988. *Grammar Practice Activities: A practical guide for teachers*. Cambridge: Cambridge University Press.
van Lier, L. 1988. *The Classroom and the Language Learner*. London: Longman.
VanPatten, B. 1995. Cognitive aspects of input processing in second language acquisition. In *Studies in Language Learning and Spanish Linguistics: In Honor of Tracy D. Terrell*, ed. P. Hashemipour, R. Maldonaldo, and M. van Naerssen, 170–183. New York: McGraw-Hill.
VanPatten, B. 1996. *Input Processing and Grammar Instruction in Second Language Acquisition*. Norwood, NJ: Ablex.
VanPatten, B., and T. Cadierno. 1993. Explicit instruction and input processing. *Studies in Second Language Acquisition* 15: 225–243.
VanPatten, B., and S. Oikkenon. 1996. Explanation versus structured input in processing instruction. *Studies in Second Language Acquisition* 18: 495–510.
Vigil, N., and J. Oller. 1976. Rule fossilization: A tentative model. *Language Learning* 26: 281–295.
Weiqing, Gu. 2004. *Input, Interaction and Second Language Learners*. Ph.D. Dissertation of Shanghai International Studies University. www.cnki.net.
Wenjun, Ni. 2004. *Effects of Recasts on Correcting English Grammatical Errors*. Master Thesis of Zhejiang Normal University. www.cnki.net.
White, L. 1987. Against comprehensible input: The input hypothesis and the development of L2 competence. *Applied Linguistics* 8: 95–110.
White, L. 1991. Adverb placement in second language acquisition: some effects of positive and negative evidence in the classroom. *Second Language Research* 7: 133–161.
White, L., N. Spada, P. Lightbown, and L. Ranta. 1991. Input enhancement and L2 question formation. *Applied Linguistics* 12: 416–432.
Wolfe-Quintero, K. 1996. Nativism does not equal universal grammar. *Second Language Research* 12: 335–373.
Young, R., and B. Yandell. 1999. Top-down versus bottom-up analyses of interlanguage data: A reply to Saito. *Studies in Second Language Acquisition* 21: 477–488.

Printed by Printforce, the Netherlands